HENRY SYLVESTER WILLIAMS AND THE ORIGINS OF THE PAN-AFRICAN MOVEMENT 1869-1911

CONTRIBUTIONS IN AFRO-AMERICAN
AND AFRICAN STUDIES
Series Advisor: Hollis R. Lynch

The Oratory of Negro Leaders: 1900-1968
Marcus Hanna Boulware
Black Labor in America
Milton Cantor, editor
The Black Teacher and the Dramatic Arts: A Dialogue, Bibliography,
and Anthology
William R. Reardon and *Thomas D. Pawley,* editors
Refugees South of the Sahara: An African Dilemma
Hugh C. Brooks and *Yassin El-Ayouty,* editors
Bittersweet Encounter: The Afro-American and the American Jew
Robert G. Weisbord and *Arthur Stein*
The Black Infantry in the West, 1869-1891
Arlen L. Fowler
The Decline and Abolition of Negro Slavery in Venezuela, 1820-1854
John V. Lombardi
A Bio-Bibliography of Countee P. Cullen, 1903-1946
Margaret Perry
The Abbé Grégoire, 1787-1831: The Odyssey of an Egalitarian
Ruth F. Necheles
Political Philosophy of Martin Luther King, Jr.
Hanes Walton
The American Slave. Series 1, Vols. 1-7; Series 2, Vols. 8-19
George P. Rawick
Nigeria, Dilemma of Nationhood
Joseph Okpaku, editor
Private Black Colleges at the Crossroads
Daniel Thompson
Ebony Kinship: Africa, Africans, and the Afro-American
Robert G. Weisbord
Slavery and Race Relations in Latin America
Robert Brent Toplin, editor
No Crystal Stair: Black Life and the *Messenger,* 1917-1928
Theodore Kornweibel, Jr.
"Good Time Coming?": Black Nevadans in the Nineteenth Century
Elmer R. Rusco

HENRY SYLVESTER WILLIAMS AND THE ORIGINS OF THE PAN-AFRICAN MOVEMENT, 1869-1911

Owen Charles Mathurin

WITHDRAWN

Contributions in Afro-American and African Studies,
Number 21

GREENWOOD PRESS
Westport, Connecticut • London, England

Library of Congress Cataloging in Publication Data

Mathurin, Owen Charles.
    Henry Sylvester Williams and the origins of the pan-African movement,
1869-1911.

    (Contributions in Afro-American and African studies ; no. 21)
    Bibliography: p.
    Includes index.
    1. Pan-Africanism. 2. Williams, Henry Sylvester, 1869-1911. I. Title. II. Series.
DT31.M36   320.5'4'0924 [B]   75-35348
ISBN 0-8371-8594-7

Library of Congress Catalog Card Number: 75-35348
ISBN: 0-8371-8594-7

First published in 1976

Greenwood Press, a division of Williamhouse-Regency Inc.
51 Riverside Avenue, Westport, Connecticut 06880

Printed in the United States of America

To Amy and Our Dutiful Daughters,
Rosemary, Barbara, and Erica

Contents

Preface

Henry Sylvester Williams has been mentioned in most articles or books on Pan-Africanism, but the comments on him are all variations on a single phrase. Williams was

"A young student."—Benito Sylvain, 1901.
"A young barrister of London, England, that conceived the idea of a convocation of Negro representatives from all parts of the world."—Bishop Alexander Walters, 1917.
"A black West Indian barrister practicing in London."—W.E.B. Du Bois, 1946.
"A young West Indian barrister in London."—Rayford Logan, 1960
"A Trinidad Barrister . . . who, so far as is known, was the first to talk about Pan-Africanism." —Colin Legum, 1961.
"A barrister-at-law from Trinidad who had made fraternal contacts with African students and leaders in London."—Richard B. Moore, 1965.
"The Trinidadian . . . who is said to have been the originator of the 1900 Pan-African Conference in London. He is very much a mysterious figure." —George Shepperson, 1966.

The Frenchman Philippe Decraene and Williams's fellow countryman George Padmore gave Williams just a little more attention. But no one has done him justice by taking proper note of his brief, interesting, and restless career.

At Williams's death his obituary predicted that his name would long be remembered by his own people for his efforts in their behalf. But sixty years later, very few among them know his name, and there is no monument to him.

My writing of his biography was seriously handicapped by the limited amount of material readily available. There are, for example, few
letters and personal documents and writings. Nevertheless my search
over a period of years has produced a considerable fund of information
with which to reconstruct for the first time the origins of the Pan-
African movement and Williams's subsequent efforts to develop it.

I have tried to recapture some of the outstanding events of his for-
mative years in the British colony of Trinidad, West Indies, which may
have shaped his thinking. It was a period in which, at least for a few
years, the island continued to be "in a state of turmoil," according to
the testimony of the United States consul, Moses Sawyer, in his report
dated June 1889. There were the movements for franchise reform and
judicial reform. But more important in the context of the life of the
black Trinidadian were two events that had the effect of heightening
black consciousness and fostering black self-respect.

One was the black-white clash over the 1888 celebration of the
"Jubilee of the Extinction of Slavery in Trinidad," which ranged the
governor, his officials, the other whites, and the coloreds against those
blacks who were decried as "a handful of boys." The other was the controversy generated by publication of James Anthony Froude's
Negrophobe travel book, *The English in the West Indies* (1888). Indeed there is to be found a germ of the Pan-African idea in the antidote
to Froude—the book, *Froudacity, West Indian Fables by James
Anthony Froude Explained,* written by a Trinidadian schoolmaster,
J. J. Thomas. Some of the personalities who were involved in the emancipation jubilee controversy were to be associated with Williams when,
thirteen years later, he returned on a visit to Trinidad bearing the torch
of Pan-Africanism.

By tracing his career from the obscurity of a youthful country
schoolmaster in rural Trinidad in the late 1880s and early 1890s to the
limelight of Victorian London at the dawn of the twentieth century
when he convened the first meeting of black men and women from many
lands to discuss the plight of their oppressed race, we can see better the
origins of the Pan-African movement.

Hitherto all discussion of Pan-Africanism has centered on Dr. W. E. B.
Du Bois, who did not tell the whole story during a long life of prolific
writing. Now it is possible to redress the imbalance by presenting the semi-
nal role of Williams and of the Haitian Benito Sylvain as well as of

others who, with Williams, organized the African Association and called the 1900 Pan-African Conference.

Thus much that is new is bared. Although the Pan-African Association lapsed in a comparatively short time, Williams had scattered the seed of Pan-Africanism in Jamaica and Trinidad. From his activities there, in London, in South Africa, and in Liberia, it is possible to glean what Pan-Africanism meant to the man who called the world's first conference of blacks.

That it meant to him, among other things, the migration of New World blacks to Africa might come as a surprise to those who recall Du Bois's bitter denunciation of Marcus Garvey and his "crazy" (Du Bois's word) back-to-Africa plan. For, well before Garvey, Williams, in a newsletter to Garvey's mentor, Dr. J. Robert Love, had proposed that Jamaican blacks should emigrate to Liberia instead of to Latin American republics. He advocated not a general exodus but the founding of what he called a "national home for the Negro race" to which New World blacks with the pioneering spirit would contribute their skills and modest capital.

I hope that this study will arouse a new interest in the pioneer of Pan-Africanism who has been a most neglected figure. If it helps to make him known especially among Africans at home and in the diaspora, this tribute of a fellow national will not have been in vain.

I am especially indebted to Mr. Henry F. Sylvester Williams for the loan of personal documents and for helpful conversations, and to my daughter Barbara Mathurin for unfailing help in obtaining material in London, England.

It is not possible to acknowledge the help of all those who have been of assistance to me during the years of labor, for they are so many; however, I must give thanks to the following for replies to enquiries and for helping to procure material:

Daphne K. Vidal-Smith, Dr. Elsa V. Goveia, Professor Lloyd E. S. Braithwaite, Linnette Vassell, Jean M. Lopez, Patricia Dunn, Ettle Francis, and G. L. Smith (Jamaica);

Rupert A. Gittens, Monica Olivier, Errol D. S. Braithwaite, Rt. Hon. Sir Hugh Wooding, TC, PC, CBE, QC, Faye McIntyre (Trinidad and Tobago);

The Registrar, Dalhousie University; the Provincial Archivist, Halifax,

N.S.; the Dominion Archivist, Ottawa; Lucy A. C. Fields, Ottawa (Canada);

Dorothy B. Porter, Dr. Herbert Aptheker, Ronald Wooding-Cooke (United States);

W. G. Penn, public relations officer, Greater London Council; Goss Bilson, secretary, National Liberal Club; Maureen Alexander-Sinclair, assistant secretary, Anti-Slavery Society; B. M. Cocks, librarian, Gray's Inn, and his successor, P. C. Beddingham; Leslie B. Frewer, superintendent, Rhodes House Library, Oxford; the Registrar, University of London King's College; Anthony Speaight, secretary, Oxford Union Society, Oxford (England).

I owe a debt of gratitude to the staffs of the following depositories and libraries:

Trinidad Public Library, Trinidad and Tobago Central Library, Parliament Library, and Registrar General's Division of the Office of the Attorney General and Ministry of Legal Affairs (Trinidad and Tobago); West India Reference Library, Institute of Jamaica (Jamaica); Library of Congress, Moorland Collection, Howard University, Washington, D.C., the New York Public Library (United States); British Museum, London, Nesspaper Library, Colindale, *Times* Library, London, and Rhodes House Library, Oxford (England).

Dr. Hollis R. Lynch, professor of history, Columbia University, New York, encouraged me from the very beginning of my study and offered a valuable critique of an earlier draft of this work; he also edited the present version. Dr. George Shepperson, department of history, University of Edinburgh, Scotland, heard indirectly of my work and wrote letters of encouragement and advice. Dr. A. P. Walshe of Notre Dame's African studies program put me in touch with Dr. Imanuel Geiss of the department of history, University of Hamburg, Germany, who very kindly sent me his microfilms of the report of the Pan-African Conference, 1900. Dr. Lynch referred me to Dr. Brinsley Samaroo of the social science faculty, University of the West Indies, St. Augustine, Trinidad and Tobago, who devoted much time and attention to reading and criticizing the manuscript. Without Dr. Lynch's help, advice, and encouragement I might not have persisted. I alone, however, am responsible for any deficiencies.

I am also very grateful to Patricia Borel of the Trinidad and Tabago Embassy, Washington, D.C., for typing the first draft and to Anne

Pantin, Port-of-Spain, Trinidad, for typing the final manuscript with exemplary care and patience.

Without the hospitality and unfailing kindness of my old friends Carey and June La Corbiniere, New York City, I might not have been able to complete the task satisfactorily. There could not have been truer friends.

OWEN C. MATHURIN

Port-of-Spain
December 1974

Biographical Outline

Henry Sylvester Williams

1869
February   Born Arouca, Trinidad, West Indies

1866   Graduated from normal school

1887   Appointed headmaster of rural school

1891   Emigrated to the United States

1893   Enrolled Dalhousie University law faculty, Halifax, N.S., Canada

1896   Arrived in London, England; entered King's College

1897
September 24   Formed African Association

December 10   Enrolled as law student, Gray's Inn

1900
July 23-25   Pan-African Conference met in Westminster Town Hall, London

August 6, 7, 8 Attended Anti-Slavery Congress, Paris

1901
March-July   Visit to Jamaica and Trinidad as general secretary, Pan-African Association; branches established

April   Pan-African Association dissolved in London in Williams' absence

August 7-9	Attended fourth annual meeting, National Afro-American Council, Philadelphia, Pa.
September 4	Arrived in London with Bishop Walters
September 13	Meeting of Pan-African Association at South Place Institute, London, summoned by Walters and Williams, revived Pan-African Association
October	First issue of *The Pan-African*

1902

| June 11 | Called to the bar by Gray's Inn; began practice as barrister |

1903

| September | Emigrated to South Africa |
| October 29 | Enrolled as advocate, Bar of the Cape of Good Hope; began practice as advocate |

1904   Visit to Basutoland as guest of King Lerothodi

1905   Returned to London to seek selection as Liberal parliamentary candidate

1906

| November 2 | Elected councillor, St. Marylebone Borough Council, London |

1908

January-February	Visited Liberia at invitation of President Barclay; addressed annual meeting of Liberian National Bar Association
	Visited Guinea and Sierra Leone before returning to London
August 28	Arrived in Trinidad from London

1911

| March 26 | Died |

HENRY
SYLVESTER
WILLIAMS
AND THE
ORIGINS OF THE
PAN-AFRICAN
MOVEMENT
1869-1911

A Feeling for Africa 1

A knowledge of the environment and the times in which he was born and of the people among whom he was reared is necessary to an understanding of Henry Sylvester Williams's feeling for Africa. Williams was born in Arouca, Trinidad, British West Indies, in 1869. The village he came from had been established in 1847 by former slaves who had bought lots of land from the state. According to the Emancipation Act of 1833, these people ceased to be the property of their masters on August 1, 1834, but they continued as apprentices bound to work for them without pay for three-fourths of their working week and for the remaining one-fourth at stipulated wages. The lash, the jail, and the treadmill were still controlled by their former masters.[1] Initially they were to be apprentices until August 1, 1840, but the period of apprenticeship for field laborers was actually terminated on August 1, 1838. Neither the Trinidad planter class nor the Colonial Office wanted to create a class of peasant farmers out of the apprentices. Their "real happiness," in the opinion of Lord Howick, Under-Secretary of State for the colonies, required that "the facility of acquiring land could be so far restrained as to prevent them on the abolition of slavery, from abandoning their habits of regular industry."[2] The policy of the British government, as of the planter-dominated Trinidad legislature, was that land be sold in large blocks well beyond the purchasing capacity of the freedman.[3] The village lots sold for $50 to $80 each to the former apprentices were in the shadow of the sugar estates and so small that to subsist freedmen had to work on the estates.

In 1869, when Williams was born, Arouca was a sleepy place. By the time he had grown to manhood, it still did not have a telephone. And only in 1876 when the railway linking Port-of-Spain with the town of Arima was built, with an intervening stop at Arouca, did the villagers have a somewhat modern mode of travel to and from the capital. Until then they had to trudge on foot or, depending on their means, ride a horse, donkey, or mule, or drive a cart or buggy into Port-of-Spain.

The villagers were mainly of African descent. They owned their small homes. Some owned or rented land away from the village where they grew food crops, cocoa, or coffee, while others worked on the neighboring estates. In the immediate vicinity of the village were such estates as St. Clair, Bon Air, Laurel Hill, and Golden Grove and Garden, owned by English or Scotch proprietors. These estates grew sugar cane with the help of indentured Indian immigrants who were housed in estate barracks. Africans worked mainly in the sugar mill and as carpenters, masons, and wheelwrights. The managers and overseers, recruited from Great Britain, were whites.

There were three elementary schools in the village—government, Roman Catholic, and Presbyterian. There were also an Anglican church served by the clergyman from the neighboring village, Tacarigua, a Scots Presbyterian kirk, and a Roman Catholic church, each with its resident minister, and a police station where a visiting magistrate held periodic, court sittings. Unlike the other ministers, the Presbyterian clergyman, Jamaica-born Rev. William Fraser Dickson, was of mixed African descent. Popular with the villagers of all faiths from his arrival in 1862, Dickson spent his whole ministry in Arouca; he became Williams's lifelong friend and his supporter in the Pan-African Association. He built the first Presbyterian church in the village and opened the first Presbyterian school in his own home.[4]

At Williams's birth slavery had been abolished for only thirty-five years. There were still people alive when he was growing up who had made the "middle passage" and others who had been born in slavery in Trinidad.

Still others had come to Trinidad as "recaptives." Many of these Africans were taken from slave ships by the Royal Navy's antislave squadron and transported to Sierra Leone for settlement. After the West Indian emancipation, plantation labor became scarce and expensive, and British sugar began to be undercut by cheaper, slave-grown sugar from Cuba and Brazil. The planters urged that Sierra Leone be tapped as a source of cheap labor, and Governor Sir Henry MacLeod despatched Robert Guppy, an English barrister connected with the sugar interests, to Sierra Leone to explore this prospect. Guppy reported that the interests of the planters would best be served by removing incentives to settlement in Sierra Leone and, instead, applying them to emigration to the West Indies.

The idea met with favor in London as well as Freetown, and the British government sanctioned recaptive labor emigration to Trinidad, British Guiana, and Jamaica. Although strict rules were devised to ensure no recaptive was coerced into going and government officials could neither encourage nor discourage emigration, the planters could send their own labor recruiting agents. These agents were well received in Freetown, and many recaptives volunteered, attracted by the prospect of higher wages. Others were reassured by the promise of a free return passage. Later this was rescinded, and some who had been induced to come to the West Indies voluntarily could not return. Others, of course, prospered and decided to make the islands their home.

There were still other Africans who, having fallen into the hands of the antislave squadron, were brought to Trinidad either from St. Helena or, under the antislavery treaties, from Havana or Rio de Janeiro where they had been emancipated. On arrival in Trinidad, however, they were put into apprenticeship. Between 1841 and 1867, a total of 8,385 recaptives and liberated Africans landed in Trinidad.[5] Thus, there were many in Williams's village who remembered Africa and yearned to return there. Among these were members of "the Nation or Tribe of Mandingo," who asked the British government in 1838 to be sent back home to Africa. They had redeemed themselves, they said, from the "House of Bondage" even before abolition; they signed their petition in Arabic characters.[6] Their dream of returning home was never fulfilled; they were not as fortunate as their fellow Muslim, Abu-Bakr-al-Siddiq of Timbuktu, who returned to Africa in 1835 after thirty years of slavery in Jamaica.[7]

During Williams's early manhood, and even at the turn of the century, the descendants of the slaves were still being called Africans. Their adoption of Christianity notwithstanding, some of them organized or participated in African ceremonies, dances, and feasts. Tribal differences of language and custom and consciousness of place of origin had largely faded where they had not disappeared under the policy of cultural genocide applied by the colonial rulers.

It is remarkable, however, that to this day African values persist, most notably among people who claim descent from the Yoruba of western Nigeria—or "Yaraba," as an 1891 newspaper described one of them charged with "practicing obeah." They identified their African gods with the saints of the Roman Catholic church and were thus able to envisage them as emanating out of the everyday world about them. The numbers of devotees of African cults do not appear in census returns for many belonged to a Christian denomination while secretly practicing the African form of worship known in Trinidad as Shango, after the Yoruba god of thunder.

The chronicler Lewis Osborn Inniss, a friend of Williams, tells of the passing of legislation in 1884 against the beating of the "big African drum to which the bass people[8] were fond of dancing calindas (a most indecent performance) on account of the noise it made." [9] What Inniss, a pillar of the English Baptist church, considered indecent may well have been the expression of the desire for fertility as practiced in African cults. But the Irish inspector of police, John Nelson Brierly, who was closely connected with the drafting of the law, said the big African drum was banned less for the noise it made than "to suppress these 'Belair' dances . . . with their accompanying orgies." In fact, the law banned the assembly in so-called disorderly yards of "convicted felons, persons convicted of riot or affray, rogues and vagabonds, and other bad characters." It required the owner of a yard in which a dance was to be held to procure a police license, and he was held responsible if any "undesirable" persons were found on the premises. [10] But so wedded were some Africans to their bamboulas (drum dances)—for example, the jouba—that they held them in defiance of the law.[11] One held in Williams's village on the Easter Monday holiday in 1891 following refusal of a police license resulted in a riot when the village policemen seized the drums, stopping the frolic. Twelve policemen were injured when reinforcements were called in, and some of the revellers arrested were sent to prison for terms ranging from two years to five years.

A remarkable feature of these revelries, in which the participants were those who felt closest to Africa, was that the singing was in French Creole, then the common tongue of the bulk of native Trinidadians, and not the English of the white officials, of business intercourse, of public instruction, and of the black immigrants from the English-speaking islands to the north. Even the newspapers and the preachers in the Roman Catholic church made the concession to the Francophiles. The former printed a section in French, sometimes in Spanish for the descendants of the original Spanish settlers and those who had joined them from neighboring Venezuela, and the preachers, who were mostly French, delivered sermons in French. While Trinidad was an English colony, the French influence was pervasive; before the English conquest in 1797, the Spanish governor had induced free French Roman Catholics, white and colored, with offers of generous grants of fertile land, the acreage given to each man increasing with the number of slaves he brought in. Later still, another exodus from the French islands to the north had entered Trinidad, fleeing the French Revolution, and there were other French immigrants too who brought with them the concept of liberty, equality, and fraternity and disturbed the society. So in the year of Williams's birth and for a long time afterwards, the French language and French Creole were dominant among the Roman Catholics who formed the bulk of the population and who were mainly black.

The two most powerful sections of the colonial society were the senior civil servants and "their natural social group"—those other whites with whom it was acceptable to consort—"the wealthy planting and commercial section of the community."[12] Men in Creole families had attended public schools in England, and British civil servants often married into the leading white Creole families or vice versa. Some of the colored, the offspring of illicit unions between European and African, were sent to schools in Britain or France by their fathers; they occupied an intermediate position between the upper classes and the Negroes and Indians. With the local upper classes so closely connected, it was difficult to ensure the impartiality of the colonial administration between rich and poor. The European civil servants felt no special responsibility to the black mass of the population, whom they despised and deprecated. But there was special protection for the indentured immigrants brought from India to work on the sugar estates— a protection supervised rigidly by the Colonial Office in London under constant prodding from the India Office.

The life-style affected by the wealthier French Creoles can be best exemplified by the merchant and planter Leon Agostini who entertained visiting English princes with a grand ball and illuminations and other preparations "upon a grand scale, the cost running . . . into the tens of thousands."[13] He spent vacations at Frankfurt on the Main and conceded, at his examination in bankruptcy, that it might be that he had lived more extravagantly than he ought to have done.[14]

The English colonial rulers took up with a will the task of making Trinidad less African and less French and more English. But Africa was very much in the news in Williams's youth and early manhood. The black continent was being explored and partitioned by the European powers, and its fabled wealth was being bared. The partitioning of the West Coast began in 1884; King Jaja of the Opobo was exiled to the West Indies in 1887; and Cecil Rhodes's British South Africa Company was chartered in 1889. The deposed king's place of exile was only 178 miles from Trinidad—the island of St. Vincent. The literate few read the local newspapers, the daily foreign news bulletins on the public board at the cable office in Port-of-Spain, and English or French magazines and newspapers at the library. They would have passed the word of King Jaja's arrival at Grenada aboard H.M.S. *Icarus* and of the criticism of the hurried decision that he should be landed instead in St. Vincent to the disappointment of the waiting crowd of blacks.[15]

For many of the black people of Trinidad, Africa was near. Those who belonged to the Church of England, like Williams and his family, would have heard and perhaps contributed to the funds raised for the support of the West Indian Mission on the Rio Pongo in West Africa. The West Indian Church Association had been founded in 1855 at Codrington College, Barbados, an institution for the training of clergy, by an Englishman, Reverend Richard Rawle, and others. They had felt the want of "missionary zeal" in the West Indies, and their aim was "to leaven" the West Indian dioceses with missionary feeling. One of Rawle's black Barbadian pupils, Reverend Philip Henry Douglin, after serving seventeen years with the Rio Pongo Mission, told a meeting in San Fernando on August 1, 1888, that it was the duty of every African man in Trinidad to help in Africa's conversion. They were to stir up "a great re-action, opposite in direction as in character to a traffic by which these colonies were peopled, sending back to Africa, as missionaries, the descendants of those who were brought over as slaves."[16] The Europeans had been withdrawn altogether in 1863 and the field left to the clergymen of African descent.

But Africa was nearer still to black Trinidadians; an African prince, the son of the king of Asante, lived five years in Trinidad under the care of the superintendent of the normal school that Williams attended in Port-of-Spain. Thus black Trinidadians knew there were African kings and princes in the land of their ancestors though they heard sung only the praises of white royalty.

Trinidad was a crown colony, which meant, according to Hume Wrong, a colony in which "the Crown retains real control of the executive." [17] It did not have representative government during Williams's lifetime nor for a long time afterward. All power lay in the hands of the governor, who was a benevolent autocrat, carrying out policy laid down by the secretary of state for the colonies, a member of the English Parliament in London. The governor presided over the legislative council consisting of his officials, who were in the majority, and nonofficials consisting of white planters and merchants chosen by the governor. The system was devised for tropical colonies peopled by blacks who were allowed no voice in the conduct of affairs. It gave rise to continuing dissatisfaction, and there was periodic agitation for self-government. As persistently as the articulate colored middle-class people demanded recognition of the right of those who paid taxes to representation, just as persistently was their demand denied by the British government.

Tired and disgusted by the repeated rejection of their demands for an "English Constitution," a group of colored people had chartered a schooner, loaded it with supplies, and left in 1852 to found a "Communist" colony in Venezuela. [18] The failure of Numancia, so called after the French-educated leader, Georges Numa Dessources, did not dampen the demands for reform in which Williams and other young black men were to become interested. Misgovernment was rife, and there was increasing danger of alienation of the ruled from their rulers. On the opening day of the carnival in 1881 a clash between police and maskers in Port-of-Spain had resulted in the wounding of twenty-eight policemen and the arrest of a number of maskers. The police commandant, Arthur Whybrow Baker, an Asante war veteran, had, without orders and without warning, tried to stop the custom of cannes brulées, a torchlight procession reminiscent of the days of slavery when the slaves were called to put out cane fires on neighboring estates.

Baker figured in another disturbance in 1884 with more serious consequences. In the Hosea riots the police Baker was leading killed twelve Indians and wounded more than one hundred others. Indians from neighboring estates were entering the town of San Fernando as had been their custom, though new regulations had been proclaimed requiring them to confine their Mohurrun or Hosea observances to the estates. The regulations had been imposed without explanation, and although the governor of Jamaica, Sir Henry Norman, an old India hand, who

conducted the subsequent inquiry, did not condone the Indians' defiance of the regulations, he emphasized the absence of any attempt to
establish rapprochement between rulers and ruled.

Fuel was added to the flames in 1887, when James Anthony Froude,
the Regius Professor of Modern History at Oxford University, after a
three-day visit to Trinidad as the guest of Attorney General Stephen
Gatty, wrote a book on his West Indian travels in which he derided
Trinidadians and their aspirations to self-rule. Froude thought that the
black and brown people of Trinidad should be quite content to pay
taxes and stand aside while whites, whom they did not elect, determined
how the revenue should be spent. "He considered a constitution with a
black minister and a black legislature" unthinkable. In fact, the leaders
of the movement for reform whom Froude maligned included, on his
own admission, some of the leading merchants of Port-of-Spain, white
and colored, who put their views the following year to the Royal
Franchise Commission headed by Froude's host, Gatty.

Froude's book, *The English in the West Indies*, gave rise to protest;
and the refutation by the Trinidadian teacher and philologist John Jacob
Thomas, published in England in 1889 and in the United States in 1890,
was warmly received in Trinidad, where in 1869 he had published a
scholarly yet nationalist work, *The Theory and Practice of Creole
Grammar*. In *Froudacity: West Indian Fables by James Anthony
Froude,* Thomas questioned Froude's truthfulness and prudence, replied to his libels, exposed the inefficiency of colonial officialdom, and
boldly proclaimed that the crown colony system was doomed. In this he
was premature, but his thesis was widely accepted in Trinidad as is evi-
denced by subsequent demands for self-rule. Contradicting Froude's
assertion that there had been no previous agitation for reform, Thomas
observed that "any respectable, well-informed inhabitant . . . who happened
not to be an official 'bird of passage.' might . . . have informed him that
Trinidad is the land of chronic agitation for Reform." But Froude's view
that black people could not be entrusted with self-government became an
article of faith with the English politicians and officials in the Colonial
Office who had the political destiny of Trinidad and its people in their
hands. [19]

Williams himself was to realize this later on when, having been inspired in his youth by the preachings of a French Creole reformer,
Philip Rostant, he tried to press once again on the Colonial Office the

case for reform of the Trinidad legislature. [20] Rostant's weekly, *Public Opinion,* advocated liberal causes, especially political and judicial reform, and it was a great influence on the young men of the day. Rostant was connected with and encouraged two organizations to which Williams belonged—the Elementary Teachers' Union and the Trinidad Literary Association—and gave generous publicity to their activities. [21] Williams was to be an apt pupil; years later, in recalling Rostant's fight for reform, he reiterated the line that crown colony rule was damaging to Trinidad and that people who had paid taxes had the right to a voice in their own government. [22]

Rostant and the mayor of Port-of-Spain, Francis Damian, a retired solicitor of Italian descent who had been chairman of the "great Reform meeting" of which Rostant had been secretary, lent their prestige to the Trinidad Literary Association, the one as vice-president, the other as president. They were in fact white patrons and elder counselors to the young membership, who fell within the category of assiduous "young negroes and colored men" who, in contrast to their "indolent and so careless" amusement-loving white counterparts, studied "half the night." [23] However, in 1888 even the progressive Rostant came in conflict with the young blacks of the Gray's Inn Literary Association over the celebration of the jubilee of the end of slavery and apprenticeship in Trinidad. The association was led by law student Edgar Maresse-Smith, Williams's friend and future collaborator in the Pan-African Association. The controversy, conducted at some length in the newspapers, is of some importance because it contributed to the sharpening of black consciousness during 1888 and 1889. [24]

Maresse-Smith and his group had initiated the idea of a public celebration of black freedom but, failing to get the timely support of people like Rostant and Damian whom they approached, proceeded on their own; the result was that there were separate jubilee celebrations. The governor, Sir William Robinson, to begin with, had refused to declare August 1, Emancipation Day, a public holiday when Maresse-Smith, at the head of a delegation of young blacks, asked for it. He was denounced by Maresse-Smith as one of a line of Negro-hating governors. [25] The governor, who rated the occasion not of sufficient importance to warrant a holiday, gave his patronage to and presided over a dinner arranged by Rostant and Conrad Frederick Stollmeyer.[26] The Maresse-Smith dinner was held under Douglin's chairmanship and had the larger attendance.

Chief Justice Gorrie was the only white official who attended both functions, being the subject of formal toasts by Maresse-Smith and Alexander
Pulcherie Pierre[27] when he arrived during the speeches.

The significance of the widely publicized controversy was twofold.
It was a conflict over the leadership between blacks and whites—who had
been the unchallenged leaders of movements—and, at the same time, it
was one between young and old; the older group, through the pen of
Rostant, denounced the assertive and self-reliant young blacks as a "handful of boys." But it is noteworthy that Maresse-Smith and such persons
as Pierre, Douglin, C. E. Petioni [28] and Emmanuel M'Zumbo Lazare,
who were either on the black side of the jubilee celebrations controversy
or in the Gray's Inn Literary Association, were to be among Williams's
collaborators in the Pan-African Association.

In 1886 there had been a sharp public quarrel between Thomas and
Rostant, but it was to Rostant that Thomas turned for aid when, in poor
health and short of cash in London in January 1889, his publisher called
for money to publish his reply to Froude. T. Fisher Unwin would not
undertake the risks of publication because the book was so specifically
a defense of the "negroes and half castes" that he would "expect *them*
to guarantee it." [29] Earlier, Rostant had thought that instead of wasting
his time and talents on two pamphlets of satirical verse, Thomas should
have been writing a great work of fiction based on Trinidad's history.
Now he evidently thought the reply to Froude a more worthwhile under-
taking, and he launched a drive for funds. With the help of the Trinidad
Literary Association he set up a committee with Mayor Damian as
treasurer to raise a sum not exceeding £140. The Trinidad Literary
Association canvassed subscriptions for it, but it is certain that it was
read by many more than the four hundred subscribers who answered
the call. The book left no doubt of Thomas's own pride in his blackness
and his interest in the fortunes of his race, wherever its members lived.
It is not unlikely that his Pan-African thinking influenced some of his
black readers, including young Williams, then only twenty.

Great enthusiasm was generated by their appeal for subscriptions
addressed to Trinidadians and all who were interested in "the good name
of the West Indies." They made great play of the word "Froudacity,"
which Thomas had coined to mean "misrepresentations couched in nice
language so as to pass for facts." [30] "Froudacity" did not merely vindi-
cate the black people of Trinidad and the West Indies. It gives a con-

temporary picture of the period in which Williams was a young country schoolmaster.

Thomas asserted that with the exception of those oppressed blacks in the southern United States, "the vast body of African descendants" in the Western Hemisphere had sufficient opportunity to begin applying themselves "according to some fixed programme about matters of racial importance." There were, among the more than "ten millions of Africans" in the Americas, some men who were "remarkable among their fellowmen," he said, but awaiting some political agency to collect and adjust them into "the vast engine essential for executing the true purposes of the civilized African race." [31] This is remarkable thinking for a self-taught man who was to be described at his untimely death in England, shortly after his book appeared, as "one of Trinidad's brightest intellectual worthies." [32]

It is evident that although Thomas had gained a certain renown, he did not altogether feel at home in the land of his birth. Africa, the birthplace of his parents and "the cradle of our race," occupied his thoughts. Writing before European colonial rule was fully established in Africa, he held the view that black people in the Western Hemisphere would be better off on that continent. These Pan-African and back-to-Africa thoughts of Jacob Thomas were to find expression in the words and deeds of Henry Sylvester Williams.

NOTES

1. J. H. Parry and P. M. Sherlock, *A Short History of the West Indies* (London: Macmillan, 1957), p. 190.
2. Eric Williams, *History of the People of Trinidad and Tobago* (New York: Praeger, 1964), p. 190.
3. Ibid., p. 68.
4. Sarah E. Morton, *John Morton of Trinidad: Journals, Letters and Papers* (Toronto: Westminster Co., 1916), p. 245.
5. C.O. 295/112; Trinidad and Tobago Historical Society Publications, p. 81.
6. Ivor Wilks, "Abu-Bakr-al-Siddiq of Timbuktu," in Philip D. Curtin, ed., *Africa Remembered* (Madison: University of Wisconsin Press, 1967), pp. 152ff.

7. Johnson U. J. Asiegbu, *Slavery and the Politics of Liberation, 1787-1861* (London: Longmans, 1969), p. 189.

8. The people who lived in the swampy flats southeast of Port-of-Spain.

9. Lewis Osborn Inniss, *Trinidad and Trinidadians* (Port-of-Spain: Mirror Printing Works, 1910), p. 97.

10. J. N. Brierly, "The Police and the Public," in *Trinidad and Tobago Year Book* (Port-of-Spain: Government Printer, 1901), pp. 261-262.

11. The jouba was not unknown in the United States. See Vachel Lindsay's poem, "The Congo," in his *The Congo and Other Poems* (New York: Macmillan, 1915).

12. H. B. D. Johnson, "Crown Colony Government in Trinidad and Tobago, 1870-1897" (D. Phil. thesis, Oxford University, 1969).

13. Inniss, *Trinidad*, p. 98.

14. *Public Opinion*, August 10, 1886.

15. *San Fernando Gazette*, June 16, 1888, quoting *Grenada Chronicle*, June 9, 1888; see also *New Era*, July 6, 1888, quoting *St. Vincent Sentinel*, June 15, 1888.

16. *San Fernando Gazette*, August 6, 1888.

17. Hume Wrong, *Government of the West Indies* (Oxford: Clarendon Press, 1923), p.70.

18. Joseph Irving Greenidge, *Bohemian Sketches* (Port-of-Spain: Greenidge, 1937), pp. 24-25; see also Jose M. Bodu, *Trinidadiana* (Port-of-Spain: Blondell, 1890), p. 15. Two years before, George Numa Dessources, leader of the exodus, had written in an editorial in the *Trinidadian*, July 17, 1850: "Yes, rulers of Trinidad, you have left no alternative to the natives of this Island, of African descent (except those who are base enough to disown their ancestry), but to bid adieu to the place of their birth; to leave a land where loathsome prejudice is rife and European rapacity threatens a collision."

19. H. A. Will, *Constitutional Change in the British West Indies, 1880-1903* (Oxford: Clarendon Press, 1970), p. 244.

20. H. S. Williams, "Trinidad, B.W.I.," in *British America*, vol. 3, British Empire Series (London: Kegan Paul, 1900), p. 474.

21. *Public Opinion*, June 21, November 5, 1889; see also *Port-of-Spain Gazette*, January 14, 1890.

22. Williams, "Trinidad, BWI," p. 474.

23. *Public Opinion*, July 12, 1888.

24. The correspondence was carried on in *Public Opinion, New Era, San Fernando Gazette*, and *The Truth*, June-August 1888.

25. *San Fernando Gazette,* June 30, 1888. The influence of Froude's book is seen in Maresse-Smith's reference to a letter from the governor as "a long Froudish tirade . . . made on the African race."

26. Stollmeyer, wealthy retired businessman and entrepreneur of German birth, who came to Trinidad by way of the United States and England. Crusader for peace, member of the Universal Peace Union of Philadelphia, sometime reformer, Good Templar, and newspaper editor.

27. Founder of the Trinidad Literary Association, signatory of reform petition, 1886, and delegate to Pan-African Conference, 1900.

28. Originator, with Maresse-Smith, of the idea of emancipation jubilee celebrations; committee member, Gray's Inn Literary Association, of which Maresse-Smith was president.

29. *Public Opinion,* February 19, 1889, quoting critic's recommendation to T. Fisher Unwin, publisher.

30. *Public Opinion,* July 2, 1889 (address by Dr. W. E. Siccard at second anniversary meeting of Trinidad Literary Association).

31. J. J. Thomas, *Froudacity* (1889; reprint ed., London: New Beacon Books, 1969), pp. 193ff.

32. *Public Opinion,* October 18, 1889.

Growing Up   2

During Williams's youth, the African imprint was still very strong on
Trinidadian life though the ethnic composition of the population had
been undergoing gradual change well before his birth. Before the arrival
of the first indentured immigrants from India on May 3, 1845, labor
immigration had been tried from other countries—West Africa, the
United States, China, Europe, and Portuguese Fayal. When slavery was
abolished, the dominant sugar planters considered it the duty of the
British government, which had compensated them for setting free their
slaves, to obtain for them a supply of cheap agricultural labor partly at
the expense of the inhabitants of Trinidad. [1]

In 1869, the year of Williams's birth, 3,329 Indian immigrants entered the island to work on the sugar estates. At the 1871 census the
Indian population numbered 27,425 in a total population of 109,638,
which included 4,545 persons born in Africa, 1,480 born in China,
954 born in the United Kingdom, and 4,779 born in other countries.
Within twenty years, the Indian population had risen more rapidly than
the total population. At the 1891 census the Indian population numbered
70,248 in a total population of 200,028, and of these, 24,841 had been
born in Trinidad of Indian parents, 2,055 had been born in Africa,
1,006 in China, 943 in the United Kingdom, and 5,665 in other foreign
countries. In spite of this rapid rise in the Indian population it was
to be a long time before they joined the mainstream of the society
and were accorded equal rights with the rest of the community.

There had been a steady influx of new residents from the neighboring
British colonies through recruitment of labor, illegal entry, or the in-
dividual initiative of persons seeking to better their lot in life. Thus, in
1871, there were in Trinidad 13,707 persons born in neighboring
British colonies registered in the census, and though they did not keep

pace with the subsidized immigration from India, their numbers had risen to 33,180 in 1891.

Williams's family was part of this predominantly black immigrant stream. His parents came to Trinidad from Barbados, possibly under the auspices of a sugar plantation. There were sugar planters who recruited labor from Barbados in preference to labor from faraway India. Some of them looked to Barbadian immigration, it was said, as a means of saving the country from "the incubus of Coolie immigration," while at the same time saving "our sugar industry" without pauperizing the other industries of the island.[2] The argument was that the Barbadian laborer was industrious, thrifty, and independent and had no need of special treatment or protection like the Indian immigrant; moreover, each employer procured his own labor at his own expense. But the majority of the planters were unmoved by such an argument. Indian immigration was cheaper to them, and they tied the immigrant to the estate with the full backing of the law.

Williams's father, Henry Bishop Williams, was a wheelwright. The wheelwright, like the blacksmith, was important to the sugar economy. He made and repaired the wheels of the estate carts and carriages and, even off the estates, in the towns, there was work to be had, for the well-to-do had carriages; carts were plentiful for the delivery of goods, and there were livery stables with carriages and hearses for hire. Henry Sylvester Williams was the eldest child, born February 19, 1869. There were to be five others—Aurora or Soli, Violet, Ruth, Hamilton, and Rufus. Henry, sturdily built, was known to family and friends as "Bucky."[3]

It is almost legendary that Barbadian parents were always firm with their children, religious, church-going, and observant of the Sabbath, filling their children with stories of colored men in Barbados who had risen to important positions in spite of the handicap of color in a white-dominated society. The best-known success stories were about Samuel Jackman Prescod and his pupil, William Conrad Reeves.

Prescod, described as "perhaps the most intelligent public man in Barbados in the nineteenth century," edited the *Liberal* newspaper and was a politician. He and Reeves were "two outstanding colored members during the century" when "men of color" were rarely elected to the ancient House of Assembly.[4] When Prescod was first elected in July 1844 as member for Bridgetown, the *Barbadian* called his election "the eternal disgrace of the city" of Bridgetown. He was accused of devoting all his energies and ability to "the ruin" of the landed proprietors by exerting "every effort to seduce the able-bodied laborers to emigrate to Trinidad and British Guiana."[5] But the black emigrant laborer or artisan who escaped the oppression of the Barbadian white planter class and improved his position in Trinidad or British Guiana was doubtless grateful to Prescod for having enabled him to get away.

Reeves, who began as a reporter on Prescod's *Liberal,* had been able, with the financial help of friends and sympathizers, to go to London and qualify as a barrister. He had returned home in 1864 and started practice. He was elected to the assembly in 1875 and in the following year was appointed solicitor general, "a very notable promotion," Bruce Hamilton observes, "for a man of his antecedents."[6] Reeves was the son of a slave woman and a "Philadelphian" who had settled in Barbados with his two sisters in the early nineteenth century, started a small drug shop, and was later appointed doctor of a parish.[7] Finding himself in disagreement with the governor, Sir John Pope-Hennessy, over the policy of confederation of Barbados with the Windward Islands, Reeves resigned as solicitor general in 1876 shortly after the bizarre confederation riots had been put down.

Freed from the confines of office, Reeves assumed the leadership of the opposition to confederation, and it was he who found the solution to the problem of the gap between the executive and the elected assembly. He proposed the creation of an executive committee consisting of officials and members of the house to whom would be referred questions of supply and general legislation to be brought before the assembly by the government. His services brought him "financial reward, the grateful affection of his white fellow-citizens, and in the end the Chief Justiceship of Barbados—honors absolutely without parallel, at the time, for a man of color in the islands." Reeves, according to Hamilton, was "never a man of liberal opinions," his sympathy toward the African race limited to holders of property, and he revealed "a complacency about the condition of the working class exceeding that of most of his white fellow-members."[8] Yet to the Barbadian in exile in the neighboring islands, such minutiae were irrelevant; among them and among those with whom they lived his name became a household word, and when he stopped in Port-of-Spain in October 1886 on his way to Tobago on circuit as chief justice and president of the Windward Islands court of appeal, his fellow Barbadians called on him and presented an address expressing their pride in his achievements.[9]

Like the Barbadian artisans who signed Rostant's petition for constitutional reform in 1887 only to be denounced by Gatty, the chairman of the Royal Franchise Commission, [10] Williams's father may have commented to his family on Trinidad's lack of a representative legislature like that of Barbados, imperfect though the latter was.

Williams grew up at a time when the Anglican and Roman Catholic clergy were vying for control of the mind of the Trinidadian child. He and his siblings may have heard their father boast that Barbados had always been British, with the Church of England, to which he belonged, as the state church, and of its never having been under the domination of French-speaking Roman Catholics. Although Williams himself seems to have grown up without any religious intolerance, he supported state rather than denominational schools.

The Williams household spoke English, but the majority of the black residents of Arouca spoke the prevailing French Creole, which Henry spoke fluently with a fine appreciation of its nuances. For the inspector of schools, who was in charge of education in the island, the Creole tongue was anathema. It might be interesting as a philological curiosity, he said in his report for 1881-1882, but it was a serious obstruction to the education of the people; it had no literature of any value for educational purposes and its mode of utterance was a hindrance to the proper acquisition of English.

The inspector, of course, was English, prejudiced and ignorant of Creole. Yet Trinidadians would have been divided on the correctness of his analysis though many would have agreed with him that it was desirable that they should be able to use effectively the language in which the laws were written and in which the commerce and learning of the empire were recorded. Some might even have made the point that competent interpreters for French and Spanish were readily available.

The inspector's·efforts in the cultivation of the use of the English language had been rewarded, he reported, with a fair measure of success and he told of often hearing little children of Trinidadian parents "running about the streets, nay even in the cocoa woods," chattering English as fluently as their predecessors fifteen or twenty years before did Creole. Yet where English was fluently spoken, it was corrupted by the influence of the Creole pronunciation and idiom, resulting in the mispronunciation of words and sentences.

These observations would probably not have applied to the pupils of the two model schools in Port-of-Spain. (Williams was to carry out

his teaching practice at one of them when he went to normal school.)
They came mainly from the English-speaking middle and upper
classes, the children of the white and colored merchants and the
small group of mainly colored professional men. Education was not
free, and though the fees for primary schools were nominal, absen-
teeism was common for such reasons as distance from school, the
disinclination of parents to undergo the trouble and expense, and the
wages derived in rural areas from the labor of children. Another cause
was illness. In 1881, when Henry Williams was twelve years old, the
attendance of the schools was seriously impaired by "the sickness,"
which exhibited itself throughout the island. The inspector of
schools reported that "malignant fevers were epidemic." Then, too,
in rural areas especially, there were bridgeless roads and fording was
dangerous in the rainy season.

One of the model schools was for boys, the other for girls.
The principal in each was English; the staffs consisted of local male
and female trained teachers, respectively, and the teachers in
training in the normal schools. The principals of the schools combined their functions with those of superintendent of the respective
male and female normal schools. These schools were near each other
at Tranquillity and near the residences of the superintendents and
the dormitories of the normal students where Williams was to live
while a teacher in training.

The ages of instruction in model as in primary schools were from
five to fifteen years. The curriculum was the same, and at the end of
the school course the pupils were required to satisfy the examiners
in the same subjects. The model schools were better staffed and
better equipped; they were fee-paying and turned out better instructed pupils than the primary schools. Boys from the model school
were able to win some of the free exhibitions that entitled the winners
to enter the government secondary school, Queen's Royal College.
For the majority of those who did not go to QRC or the Roman
Catholic St. Mary's College, passing out of Tranquillity was the end
of formal education, which was a good basic one.

As a poor country boy, Henry went to the village government school
where he met sympathetic teachers who brought out the best in him.
At the end of the school course, he was entered as a candidate for the
normal school in Port-of-Spain for training as an elementary teacher.

As the demand for teachers fluctuated from year to year, so did the number of students admitted to the two-year training course. It required attendance at classes along with teaching in the Boys' Model School, but there was no certainty at the end of the apprenticeship that the student who passed the final examination would find a vacant headmastership immediately. In such cases he spent a third year as a normal student or took up an assistantship elsewhere until a post was available. Those who were disinclined to wait sought other employment.

When he passed the entrance examination, Williams moved to the quarters at Tranquillity where James Henry Collens, an Englishman, was superintendent of the Men's Normal School and principal of the Boys' Model School. Collens was a liberal imperialist and a Good Templar (a temperance activist) from whom Williams may have imbibed some of his passion for temperance and his feeling for empire. Williams was at the impressionable age of fifteen when he took up residence in the apartments of the students in the schools' compound, which Collens supervised from his residence close by. Like the curriculums of the schools, even the layout of the buildings in relation to one another was based on English precedent. The seven students in residence each received a small allowance while nonresidents acting as monitors were paid stipends ranging from five pounds to twenty pounds a year. Life for the students in residence—the others were more mature than Williams—must have been simple and spartan. Drinking would have been taboo with Collens's temperance leanings.

Apart from having the oversight of the male students, Collens had in his home during Williams's stay in normal school an African prince, the son of the deposed King Kofi Karikari of Asante. Prince Kofi Intim, as "a mere youth" representing his father, had signed, along with nineteen chiefs, the treaty of submission to the British at Cape Coast in March 1874. Among requests made of the British was one that Kofi Intim be sent to be educated in England. And so, according to Sir Frederick Charles Fuller, Kofi Intim "was educated at the Surrey County School and given an appointment in Trinidad, and later on, in the Gold Coast with an allowance of £120 a year."[11]

Inniss tells of Kofi Intim's arrival in Trinidad in July 1881 and of his holding a post in the Public Works Department. He describes him as "of small stature" and how a crowd usually followed him when he accompanied Collens to church. But the novelty soon wore off and people became used to seeing "the Black Prince," as they called him. [12]

Collens's black charges, who were among the brightest young people in Trinidad, must have also taken an interest in Prince Kofi Intim. Indeed, they would have conversed with him about life in his home-land and how he came to be in Trinidad; and contact with him would have stimulated an interest in the home of their ancestors, which they knew only as legend.

The students' syllabus of study was standard for an English training college. No allowance was made for their different backgrounds, no more than did the syllabus of the schools in which they would teach children in an agricultural country to be good clerks for whom jobs did not exist. At the end of their course they were examined in read-ing, dictation, English history (general outlines), English grammar, Milton's *Lycidas,* geography, school management, arithmetic, algebra, and music. [13] On the basis of such examination they obtained the certificate of competency to teach.

Williams was about seventeen years old when he sat the examin-ation in 1886 at the Boys' Model School. There were twenty-nine entrants but eight absented themselves, possibly for lack of prepara-tion. Seven of the twelve men who sat and five of the nine women were normal school students. Williams was one of only seven candi-dates who passed, being awarded a Class III certificate. He had the dis-tinction of being the only candidate certified as qualified to teach singing, and there were only eight other teachers similarly qualified in Trinidad. [14]

It was an unusual feat to qualify as a schoolmaster at seventeen years of age, so Williams had to wait until the following year to be appointed in charge of a school. It was probably during this period that he taught at Eastern Boys' Government School in Port-of-Spain. [15] Teaching was miserably underpaid. Other opportunities were not plentiful, and so young Williams had been fortunate to have been offered his chance. Others less gifted and less fortunate would have had to be apprenticed to a trade like shoemaking, tailor-ing, carpentry or masonry, or wheelmaking. Otherwise, with the right contact one might land a job as a poorly paid and overworked store or lawyer's clerk with hours lasting from dawn to dark. The few lower-paid civil service and government railroad jobs went to white and colored graduates of the boys' secondary schools, and even then they had to serve initially and indefinitely in unpaid supernumerary posts, waiting for a vacancy. Merit alone was not sufficient; the right color, family connections, and a prominent sponsor to put the timely word in the right ear were needed.

The more ambitious secondary school graduates whose parents were better circumstanced could aim to be druggists or land surveyors or solicitors—all professions for which training was available locally by apprenticeship and examination. Some who became druggists used their qualifications as a stepping stone in their ambition to study for the medical profession abroad. The men held in the highest esteem, apart from the English public officials and the merchants and planters who comprised the upper classes, were the doctors and barristers, who had to obtain their qualifications in England, Scotland, or Ireland. Even if a doctor had studied in the United States, as a few had done, he had to obtain a British qualification, and a barrister had to obtain his qualification by traveling to London and becoming a member of the English bar. But it was unusual for a Trinidadian doctor or lawyer to obtain a post in the government service; such jobs were reserved for their English counterparts. In Trinidad there were no facilities for college or university education.

Williams's attendance at normal school had given him a good beginning. Though younger than his colleagues, he was among the best of them; his name appeared in the school prize list for both the years 1884 and 1885. At the Boys' School prize-giving in 1885 he was awarded "an extra prize for the highest number of marks." He attended the 1886 award ceremony when the officer administering the government, Henry Fowler, distributed the prizes and remarked on the growth of the school from thirty pupils in 1878 to 230 in eight years. Having accomplished a rare feat of qualifying as a schoolmaster at seventeen to the delight of his parents and former teachers, "Bucky" Williams was ready to face the future.

In 1887 Williams took charge of his first school, La Fortunée-Bien Venue Government School, in the sugar belt centered on San Fernando, the island's second largest town. The estates La Fortunée and Bien Venue in Victoria County were together the largest producers of sugar of fourteen estates owned by the Glasgow firm of Charles

Tennant, Sons and Company. The two together were second only to
the Colonial Company's Usine Sainte Madeleine Estate, not far away.
In that year the two estates had 356 Indian indentured laborers, and
there were 115 boys and 76 girls, the children of Indian immigrants
not under indenture.[16] A sprinkling at least of these children would
have been among the 146 children who attended the school during the
year when the average daily attendance was only fifty-five, though it
represented an increase of nineteen over 1886. Headmaster Williams
collected ten pounds nine shillings and sixpence in school fees during
the year, which was not much of a return.[17]

An important event in the southern area occurred soon after
Williams took charge of the school. This was the induction on February 24 of a black clergyman as incumbent of St. Clement's Chapel
at St. Clement's only a few miles from Bien Venue Estate. Reverend
Philip Douglin had served as a missionary in West Africa; and
Williams came to know him and was to meet him again years later
in connection with the Pan-African Association.

Soon after Douglin's induction the local newspaper wrote of
reports "in the upper circles" in San Fernando that "the member
for Naparima has sent a protest to his Lordship the Bishop for having
appointed the Revd. Douglin to the incumbency of St. Clement's.
Three cheers for George Townsend!!!"[18] The member for Naparima—not elected by the people, for they had no franchise, but appointed by the governor to "represent" the Naparima district in the legislative council—was the Honorable George Townsend Fenwick, the
planting attorney of the Colonial Company. St. Clement's was the
chapel in which he and other white staff of sugar estates worshipped.

The new incumbent was receiving a great deal of attention. Only two
months after inducting him, Bishop Rawle, his old tutor, was back at
St. Clement's for the confirmation of thirty-five parishioners and to
bless the schoolroom that Douglin had already added to the primary
school. The *San Fernando Gazette* noted on April 30 what it called
"this new departure" at the ceremony—the absence of other clergy,
as it was the custom at confirmation services for clergy of neighboring
parishes to attend. It suggested that the absence of neighboring clergy
was because of Douglin's color and said it could not pass over in silence
the "marked indifference of those who ought to fraternise with one who,
from his birth and education, is their equal." A week later it published

what it said was an excerpt from a letter to the editor's friend from an "important country gentleman." This referred to the good work being done at St. Clement's and added: "I wish some people could learn that religion must be more than skin deep. God looks to the heart." The paper noted, apparently by way of amends, that the rector of St. Paul's, San Fernando, "did invite" Douglin to preach in his church during the Lenten season. Then, on August 1, Emancipation Day, on the invitation of the guild of St. Paul, Douglin delivered a lecture in St. Paul's Anglican School, "The River Pongas Mission," in which he described the work being done among their kinsmen in West Africa by the missionaries of African descent from the West Indies. The lecture, which was later issued as a pamphlet, received wide publicity—six columns in the *San Fernando Gazette* of August 6—as did the first harvest festival during Douglin's tenure, which was attended by well-wishers from all over Naparima.

At the end of the year Williams was sent to Canaan, which was a little nearer to San Fernando. The pupils of his former school were divided between two schools, one at La Fortunée and another at Bien Venue under separate headmasters. Canaan was smaller than the combined school had been. It was on the Canaan sugar estate owned by another absentee Scotsman, James Lamont, and run in conjunction with the Palmiste Estate. On the outskirts of Canaan Estate was Canaan Village, then commonly called "The Bamboo." It had an un-savory reputation as a haunt of idlers, gamblers, thieves, highway robbers, and ne'er-do-wells. Dozens of idlers were to be seen "under the galleries" even on Sunday "indulging in the game commonly known as seby-leby, which invariably ends in bloodshed."[19] In a plea for protection for the law-abiding, the *San Fernando Gazette* of September 21 said Canaan and Alley's Creek needed a police station.

Only eighty pupils were in attendance during the year Williams spent at Canaan, and the average daily attendance was only thirty-five, eight more than the previous year but lower than at his first school. There were fifty-two pupils on roll at the end of the year—twenty-seven boys and thirty-five girls—when the sum of four pounds had been collected in school fees. A few children of Indian immigrants may have been attending, for on Canaan Estate there were sixty-two male and twenty-one female indentured immigrants and also thirty-five male and fifty-two female ex-indentures with their children—thirty-four boys and twenty-seven girls.

Despite his youth Williams appears to have performed satisfactorily in his first two years of his career as a schoolmaster. His tasks would have included giving lessons to the staff of monitors preparing for pupil teacher or assistant teacher examinations, and he would have had to maintain relations with the parents of his pupils, his staff, and the warden who was manager of the school. The warden was the chief official of the county and, as the school's manager, might pay a visit on his rural rounds. The headmaster might also call on him on a Saturday when he went to pay in the fees at his office in San Fernando or to draw the teachers' salaries at the end of the month.

The warden apparently was impressed with young Williams for he appointed him registrar of births and deaths for the Lagoon district, ward of South Naparima West, by notice dated July 3, 1888, published in the *Royal Gazette*. It was not unusual to appoint headmasters to perform the registrations of births and deaths, though those chosen were not usually under twenty years of age as Williams was then. Schoolmasters were normally the most literate in their rural communities, and such an office would be welcome both as a source of a small supplement to their meager salaries and as another mark of official status. For young Williams this recognition must have been welcomed, and the responsibility must have quickened his self-confidence.

But Williams spent just one year in Canaan. In early 1889 he was transferred to take charge of the San Juan Government School, just a few miles east of Port-of-Spain by rail or road and much nearer to his home at Arouca. It was a rural area, with the residents mainly Roman Catholic and Creole-speaking. Père Forestier, the parish priest, was French and was referred to as the curé; when his parishioners presented him an illuminated address to mark the silver jubilee of his ordination, it was in French.

The school's annual prize day was noticed in *Public Opinion* of August 13, which described it as "a very successful entertainment." There was no mention of the headmaster but a large attendance saw "a well got up program," which included "glees, songs, recitations and dialogues" and was followed by dancing. A fuller report three days later praised Williams for the painstaking manner in which he had trained his pupils and expressed regret that such gatherings of parents, pupils, teachers, and friends were not more frequent. It ended: "Long may the present master continue to merit the praise and well wishes of the inhabitants and may the Government recognize in Mr. Williams the great benefit to the masses where there is the right man in the right place."

Williams's youth apparently was not held against him for he was then just about six months short of his twenty-first birthday, but he was not to wait for further official recognition of his merits as schoolmaster. He seems to have maintained good relations with his colleagues and had an early appreciation of the necessity for an organization to advance the cause of education and to protect the interests of teachers. In June 1889, he had attended a meeting of teachers at the Boys' Model School convened by Antoine Fortuné, headmaster of a Catholic-assisted school. The meeting agreed that a teachers' association be formed and elected Collens president and Fortuné secretary, who, with five others, were charged with drafting rules for presentation on the second Saturday in August. [20] However, it was not until the following January that the Trinidad Elementary Teachers' Union was formally launched with an address full of encouragement by the reform-minded chief justice, Sir John Gorrie. Williams, as a foundation member, attended this inaugural meeting under the chairmanship of Collens.

The prospects for Williams in teaching were not promising. About the time of his twenty-first birthday a letter appeared in the *Port-of-Spain Gazette* lamenting that young men had nothing to induce them to enter the ranks of teachers. There was no money in the profession, and in consequence they sought jobs elsewhere. Under the salary scale then in force Williams, as a male Class III teacher, received a maximum salary of sixty pounds a year. His senior male colleagues who had years of experience and had earned Class I certificates received a maximum of one hundred pounds. The scales for women teachers were lower yet.

A change made later in the year did not allay dissatisfaction. Beginning in 1891 all salaries were to be fixed. It meant an increase of fifteen pounds a year for Williams and twenty-five pounds for the top teachers. There was increased dissatisfaction as a result, and teachers said they felt they were in a worse position than before.

By this time, however, Williams was already in the United States of America. He wanted to move from teaching to something more lucrative, some profession that would give him a higher standing and satisfy the ambitions of a talented young man. So, with the blessings of his parents whom he was not to see again, and the good wishes of fellow teachers and friends, he sailed for New York.

NOTES

1. One-third of the cost of immigration was borne by the Trinidad Treasury.

2. *Public Opinion,* July 6, 1886.

3. Conversations with Mr. H. F. Sylvester Williams, November 2, November 18, 1968, Petit Valley, Trinidad, November 23, 1968, San Juan, Trinidad.

4. Bruce Hamilton, *Barbados and the Confederation Question, 1871-1885* (London: Crown Agents, 1956), p. 4.

5. Ibid., p. 7.

6. Ibid., p. 38.

7. *Mirror,* January 10, 1902; Reeves's obituary was evidently written by one who knew him from boyhood.

8. Hamilton, *Barbados,* p. 38.

9. *Public Opinion,* October 8, 1886.

10. Ibid., November 2, 1886.

11. Frederick C. Fuller, *A Vanished Dynasty, Ashanti* (London: Murray, 1921), p. 143.

12. Lewis Inniss, *Trinidad and Trinidadians* (Port-of-Spain:Mirror Printing Works, 1910), p. 98.

13. *Trinidad Royal Gazette,* November 28, 1888.

14. Ibid.

15. *Port-of-Spain Gazette,* December 19, 1909.

16. *Trinidad Royal Gazette,* June 12, 1889.

17. Ibid., November 28, 1888.

18. *San Fernando Gazette,* March 26, 1887.

19. A dice game analogous to craps in the United States and favored by gamblers; so called from the fact that if the player shoots seven ("seby") and eleven ("leby"), he wins his first roll and plays again.

20. *Public Opinion,* June 21, 1889.

Prelude to Pan-Africanism: 3
Sojourns in the
United States, Canada,
and England

Nothing is known of Williams's stay in the United States--what work he did, the kind of life he led. At twenty-two he had engaged in no other occupation than teaching, but his Trinidad certificate of competency had no value and could not open any doors to a teaching job in the United States. The jobs available to blacks were either heavy manual labor or domestic chores, which Williams found uncongenial. But because he had professional ambition, he persisted.

Life in New York City would have been quite a change to him after the monotonous, placid rural calm of Trinidad. As a newcomer he took a keen interest in the situation of Afro-Americans,[1] who were discriminated against, denied equal rights, and often lynched. He was aware of the increasing disfranchisement of the blacks in the South; in 1891 there were only three blacks in Congress.

But Williams also saw the positive side of Afro-American life. He noticed the existence of separate, independent black churches and contrasted this with Trinidad where the Christian religions were under white domination with white bishops and just one or two black clergy. These black American churches, by their very names, maintained the identification of their following with Africa. At the same time they satisfied the black need to belong while providing opportunities for development of an independent black leadership. Thus the churches played a vital role in the life of black Americans and received much publicity in the black press, which was another novel feature to Williams, for in Trinidad most newspapers were owned by whites although they catered to the general community.

The great black newspaper of the time was the weekly *New York Age* edited by Timothy Thomas Fortune, confidant of Booker T. Washington, leading black editor, and later a critic of Williams's efforts in the

Pan-African cause. [2] As editor of the *Age* and reporter on black affairs for the *New York Sun,* Fortune wielded considerable influence in the black community, both in and out of New York City. He had succeeded to the presidency of the short-lived National Afro-American League, formed in Chicago in 1889, at a national convention that he had called. Later he was an official of the successor National Afro-American Council headed by Bishop Alexander Walters of the African Methodist Episcopal Zion Church, who was to preside at the Pan-African Conference in London in 1900.

From their offices in Manhattan, Fortune and his co-publisher Jerome B. Peterson also published *Afro-American Press* and *Black Phalanx,* which they offered for joint subscription with the *Age* at special rates. [3] Fortune was then at the height of his power. Later he claimed that he was the originator of the idea of Pan-Africanism and that the young West Indian Williams seized upon it during residence in New York, bided his time, and then called the London conference. [4]

The *Age* gave much attention to black church activities, black politics, and AME Bishop Henry McNeal Turner's campaign for black emigration to Africa. It frequently mentioned the movements of the Rev. Dr. Alexander Walters, pastor of Mother Zion AME Zion Church, a popular black preacher and well known for his work in Christian endeavor. It is not known whether Williams met him at this time but they were later to be close collaborators in the Pan-African Association.

It was a time when "African fever," as it was described, was prevalent in the black communities of the South. [5] The strong desire to emigrate to Liberia manifested itself in the number of blacks who applied to the American Colonization Society for passage to Africa under its auspices and the numbers who were duped by unscrupulous promoters. Groups of them were stranded in New York City because, so eager were they to get away from the oppressive conditions of work and hard times, that they came well ahead of the scheduled time to take ship even when told there was no room for them.

With the wide publicity and the controversy surrounding it, Williams would certainly have heard of Bishop Turner's back-to-Africa plan. The *Age* attacked it as extreme although it was forced to admit that the idea had stirred up unusual interest. Turner, who was to be among race leaders whom Williams consulted before the Pan-African Conference, was advocating the emigration of "100,000 to 150,000 of the colored

race." [6] He spoke on the plan to an enthusiastic farewell meeting at
Bridge Street Church, Brooklyn, before leaving on his first visit to Africa
in October 1891. [7] On the platform was Thomas McCants Stewart,
"the colored lawyer of 81 Adelphi Street," a prominent black lawyer
active in Democratic politics and a member of the Brooklyn School
Board. Stewart had worked in Liberia and was to be associated with
Williams during a later sojourn there. [8]

Despite his criticism of Turner's plan, Fortune published Stewart's
views in favor of it. But Stewart's was a cautious approval, advising that
for any migration to succeed it must consist of the best black Americans.
He suggested that all participants, before they undertook pioneer work
in Africa, should first settle in Kansas, California, or some other western
state where they could acquire the wealth, character, and training necessary. [9]

Because of the racial barriers and the lack of congenial work, Williams
ended a two-year stay in the United States and, moving to Canada, entered Dalhousie University in Halifax, Nova Scotia, in 1893. [10] Yet,
however uncongenial the work he did in the United States may have
been, he had earned sufficient money to begin his studies.

Dalhousie was a small institution with faculties only in arts, medicine,
and law and a student body of around two hundred. It had been founded
in 1821 as Dalhousie College by the Earl of Dalhousie, lieutenant-governor of Nova Scotia, "for the education of youth in the higher branches
of science and literature." After many vicissitudes it was reorganized in
1864 and later enlarged by the addition of the faculty of medicine and
then of law. [11]

Williams was registered as a general student in the faculty of law
during the 1893-1894 session but the university records of the time are
not at all detailed and give no specific information regarding him. [12]
Thus it is not possible to find out how far he reached in his studies or
how long he pursued them. It is certain, however, that he did not gradu-
ate. He may well have chosen Dalhousie because Nova Scotia was the
Canadian province with the largest number of blacks. They were descended from four strands—the blacks who came north with their
Loyalist masters; the black pioneers who fled north from the United
States on their own; the descendants of the Jamaican Maroons who were
transported by the government of Jamaica; and the refugees who had
fought on the British side in the Revolutionary War and for whom, like

their counterparts sent to Trinidad, the British had to find a home. [13]

A biographical sketch of Williams, published in 1906 and evidently compiled from material he supplied, states that he traveled through Canada and the United States. [14] Whether this was in the course of working on the railroad or otherwise is not known. Nor is it known what friendships, if any, he formed at Dalhousie or in the black community in and near Halifax. The next that is known of him after entry into Dalhousie is his arrival in England in 1896.

Williams arrived in London in 1896 and enrolled at King's College of London University. The records of the college, "very incomplete" so far back, [15] contain no trace of his enrollment. Williams sustained himself by work as a Church of England Temperance Society official lecturer, [16] which took him to all parts of the British Isles speaking under the auspices of parish churches. He also lectured on thrift for the National Thrift Society whose chairman, Dr. Greville Walpole, wrote that Williams's heroic struggle to make ends meet won his admiration, because the "little" he was able to earn by his lectures "simply defrayed the cost of living." [17]

Like many other young men of the day devoid of means but fired with ambition to rise above the limited opportunities of their environment, he had found his way to Victorian London. London was the hub of the empire, the metropolis; it was the place where opportunity lay, where the aged Queen Victoria reigned and Parliament made laws for a vast empire.

Williams was not as fortunate as some of his fellow Trinidadians who had come to study for professions at the expense of wealthy parents or as young winners of a government scholarship who received regular remittances. He too planned to study—to read for the bar and return home to practice. But being on his own, he was under less restraint and could act more independently than most other students from Trinidad. And so he was soon taken up with events in Africa, which gave rise to protest from the humanitarians and liberal interests with which he was soon to ally himself.

Summing up the year 1896, the London monthly *Review of Reviews* said that the "Dark Continent occupied more than its fair share of the attention of the world, and especially of England." [18] It was the year after the Jameson raid, the abortive attempt by Cecil Rhodes to engineer a rising among disgruntled immigrant whites (Uitlanders) in the Transvaal to overthrow President Kruger's republican government and to bring the country and the Orange Free State into a united South Africa under British rule. Dr. Leander Starr Jameson, Rhodes's agent and administrator of Bechuanaland, was to launch an invasion with the police force of Rhodes's British South Africa Company simultaneously with the uprising. The abortive raid ended Rhodes's political career as prime minister of Cape Colony. The repercussions were being felt throughout 1896, which was marked by Jameson's trial and conviction for conspiracy. Chamberlain, the colonial secretary, had been privy to the plan but was whitewashed along with Rhodes by a House of Commons all-party committee. Yet what Jameson's raid failed to do was to be achieved by the Anglo-Boer war, which gave Britain control of the whole of South Africa.

It was the year also of the Abyssinian Emperor Menelik's crushing defeat of the Italian armies at Adowa with his volunteer peasant troops and the ensuing fall of the Italian government, precipitating riots in Italy's main cities and towns. This defeat by an African state was a stunning setback to Italy's ambition for a large African empire. The victory brought Ethiopia—then better known as Abyssinia—before the world, put pride into the breasts of Africans everywhere, and made all realize that the Emperor Menelik II was "a great sovereign worthy of respect."[19]

It was the year also of the British troops' march on Kumasi and the abduction of the Asantehene (the king of Ashanti), with the queen mother, the Asantehene's father, other members of his family, the Asante guards, and others, to Elmina, to Sierra Leone, and finally to the Seychelles in the Indian Ocean. The Asantehene's exile was to last twenty-eight years.

It was the year of the Matabele war and the Mashona revolt, which brought reports to London of the "enslaving and sjambokking of the men; the debauching of the women and young girls; the appropriation of their cattle and their mealies"[20] by the English settlers. But the English publicist William T. Stead, who edited the *Review of Reviews,* pleaded for "lenient judgement" for his fellow countrymen who were "at the front bearing the heat and burden of the day." Those like him who believed in "the civilizing mission of our race" found the accusations "the most bitter" to be borne.[21]

The queen noted in her speech at the opening of Parliament in January 1897 that the rebellion in Matabeleland and Mashonaland had been "repressed" and that the depressed condition of the sugar industry in "my West Indian colonies" had seriously affected "their prosperity." With "deep regret" she said "scarcity and famine" affected a large part of "my dominions" in India. Plague had also appeared in the seaport towns of Bombay and Karachi and showed no sign of ending. [22]

Yet at the end of January the colonial secretary, Joseph Chamberlain, announced to a happy House of Commons that he had invited the premiers of the self-governing colonies to come to London as state guests to celebrate the queen's diamond jubilee. Royal carriages would be placed at their disposal and they were asked to bring selected contingents of troops from their respective colonies to march in honor of the queen. [23] But there was a discordant note. The Irish Members of Parliament announced they could not take part in the jubilee demonstration because Ireland was governed "against the people's will" under a system growing more and more intolerable. [24]

The correspondent of the *Port-of-Spain Gazette* probably saw Jubilee Sunday, June 20, 1897, much as Williams did. London, he reported back to Trinidad, had never seen such a Sunday: the streets were like a fair, crowded with "the highest and lowest of all classes." Everybody, he said, was in holiday humor. Williams saw the Trinidad contingent march in the queen's procession: his friend, Lieutenant Lazare of the artillery with the blue-coated gunners, was among them. "Trinidad's little contingent more than held its own," the correspondence reported. [25] Williams himself saw it as "a precedent it is possible to expect from other natives." Thrilled by the pageantry, the young colonial uncritically characterized the celebrations as "a glorious occasion." [26]

The colonial premiers had all come and ridden in the royal carriages, but they were all white. Crown colonies like Trinidad or even colonies with representative institutions like Barbados did not have premiers: premiers were reserved for the white self-governing colonies or those like Cape Colony and Natal where the majority Africans were beyond the pale, disfranchised though taxed. Shortly after the jubilee, when the Liberal MP Sir Charles Dilke raised the question of extending popular representation to the West Indian colonies, Chamberlain dismissed the suggestion as premature. [27] Later, the old protagonist of imperial federation was said to have abandoned a plan for representation of the colonies in the House of Commons.

Williams met Lazare in the intervals between the engagements of the

visiting contingents and must have visited him in his quarters at Chelsea
Barracks. Lazare was a solicitor in Port-of-Spain where his father,
a Guadeloupean member of the French regiment Chasseurs d'Afrique,
had settled in Trinidad in the early part of the nineteenth century.
Williams, Lazare, and other Trinidadian friends discussed, among
other things, the position of Africans in the world in the light of the
disabilities they suffered. During the visit Lazare earned the reputation of being a conversationalist equal to any occasion. When presented to the queen, who remarked on his command of the English
language, he promptly assured her that all his countrymen spoke
English.

   Although Williams was engaged with public affairs and his lecturing,
he had not given up his ambition of reading for the bar, and he enrolled
as a student of Gray's Inn on December 10, 1897.[28] He evidently satisfied the requirements for entrance by passing a preliminary examination
in English, Latin, and history.
   His course of study covered jurisprudence (including international
law), Roman civil law, equity, real and personal property, and criminal
law. The lecturers included university professors and distinguished counsel in private practice. Attendance at lectures, held under the auspices of
of the Council of Legal Education set up by the Four Inns of Court, was
not compulsory. With examinations held four times a year, a student
could proceed at his own pace. In addition to passing the examinations,
students were required to "keep terms" by dining in the hall of their
inn.
   The treasurer's office was an important place on the Gray's Inn
premises in Holborn. There the under-treasurer operated, receiving the
fees of students, offering them advice, and managing the affairs of the
inn. Members and students could use the dining hall, whose doorway was
set in a "glorious screen" presented to the inn by Queen Elizabeth I; the
adjoining pension chamber where the benchers (members of the bench)
held their meetings (pensions); the library; the chapel; the common
room; and Gray's Inn gardens where barristers and students (and sometimes the public) strolled or sat beneath the trees. It was the haunt of
students between lectures or between stints of reading in the library.
The common room was the meeting place of barristers as well as
students of the inn where they entertained their visitors, and it was

Williams's first address as honorary secretary of the African Association.
The benchers, supervisors of the affairs of the inn, were charged with the
exercise of discipline over its members. They were judges of the High Court
or leading barristers.

Among students enrolled at Gray's Inn in Williams's time was a
fellow villager, Richard E. Phipps. Others were Charles S. René and
William Grell from Trinidad and George J. Christian from Dominica
who, like Williams, had been a schoolmaster. Phipps was the son of a
druggist and cocoa planter while René was a government scholar.
Grell came from a colored business family.

Williams must have made good progress in his legal studies at Dalhousie and at King's College. Within three months of admission at
Gray's Inn, he had passed the examination in Roman law,[29] which required a knowledge of Latin, and two months later he had passed examinations in constitutional law and legal history.[30] Thus he was left
with only the bar final to sit in the remaining two and a half years to
to complete the normal three years required to qualify for the bar.
Williams did not devote himself wholly to study; he had to earn his
living by lecturing, which involved travel to various parts of the
British Isles. He had already formed the African Association and had
fallen in love.

The best barometer for Williams's views on interracial relations is his
marriage to a white woman. He believed in the equality of the races and
not in racial exclusivity. What he wanted and advocated was equality of
treatment for all people everywhere, regardless of race. He considered
no race to be superior to the Negro race.[31]

Agnes Powell was slightly older than Williams. She worked in the
book depot of the Church of England Temperance Society at Deansgate,
Westminster, and she must have met Williams on his visits to the depot
in connection with his lecturing.[32] She was the eldest of a family of
three sons and four daughters of Captain Francis Powell and Mrs. Powell
of Gillingham, Kent. Captain Powell was prominent in local masonic and
Conservative political circles.[33]

Williams was in good spirits when, on December 20, 1897, ten days
after his admission to Gray's Inn as a law student, he wrote to "Miss
Powell"—evidently not knowing her Christian name—inviting her to tea
two evenings later. It was a somewhat tentative letter from a hesitant
would-be suitor.[34] Miss Powell probably accepted the invitation. At

any rate, three weeks later, Agnes Powell and her sister Amy were present at a social gathering of members and friends of the African Association in Exeter Hall. [35]

The friendship rapidly grew to affection and the question of marriage
arose. Mrs. Powell and Amy favored the marriage; Captain Powell opposed it strongly and would not give his consent. The fact that the
suitor was an aspirant to a learned profession made no difference. To
Captain Powell, Williams's blackness and his daughter's whiteness were
incompatible. Nevertheless, Williams and Agnes were married in 1898,
and their first child, Henry Francis Sylvester, was born in 1899. [36]

It is not known whether Williams had any qualms about the success
of his interracial marriage. At the age of twenty-nine he must have gone
into it with the determination to face any difficulties that might arise in
relation to race and color. One difficulty was that Captain Powell would
not receive him so he could not accompany Agnes on her visits home
to Gillingham.

Sometime in 1897 or 1898 Williams delivered a lecture on Trinidad
in the popular Sunday afternoon course on the British empire at South
Place Institute, Finsbury. The course, held over a period of three years
(1895-1898) consisted of over one hundred lectures, which were eventually published in five volumes. Williams and six Indians were the only
non-Europeans among the lecturers, comprising "travelers, natives, and
those to whom had been given the task of governing the various
provinces of our Empire." [37] In Williams's lecture are found some views
reminiscent of those propagated by the reformer Rostant, whose name
he mentioned and whose work in the vain quest for the franchise he
praised.

Williams proclaimed himself for representative government and
against crown colony rule, which he denounced as a "heartless system . . .which is a synonym for racial contempt." He pointed to the
racialist implications of a legislative council in Trinidad with white men
only, none of them elected, in a community in which the majority
were not white. No self-constituted body, as he put it, could represent
the needs and grievances of a people differing in customs and habits,
especially when the councillors were "separate and apart" from the
people. Under crown rule, he lamented, the subject failed to realize
his civis Britannicus sum and had no pride in his status. In unequi-

vocal language he asserted "taxation without representation is a gross crime." [38]

Williams again expressed his views on reform in Trinidad in a pamphlet, which he circulated to Members of Parliament in March 1899. [39] Judging the time opportune for a renewal of efforts to achieve a reform of the legislature, he rounded up a few Trinidadians in London to form a deputation to meet a group of MPs under the auspices of the Cobden Club, a pressure group of Liberal members of Parliament dedicated to free trade and cheap food imports. [40] Under questioning by the MPs, Williams showed that he was in close touch with events back in Trinidad.

In the March 1899 pamphlet, *The People's Case,* he had pointed out that the governor chose whom he liked to sit on the legislative council, and these usually represented the great sugar interests; the people who owned and cultivated minor crops like cocoa, coffee, fruits, and vegetables were not considered. He protested against the recent suppression of the Port-of-Spain borough council on Chamberlain's order, describing the move as "retrogressive" and demanding a "fair and impartial" hearing. The people, he said, realized the "fatuity" of the crown colony system and were asking for at least a small share of representation. The pamphlet ended with a declaration that the people as taxpayers demanded the "universal right of British subjects—representation with taxation." Williams seemed determined to ignore Chamberlain's 1895 ukase on colonial representation.

The following names appeared as signatories to the statement: H. Hamel-Smith, Snr., R. Sydney-Smith, Junior, Hon. H. A. Alcazar, Q. C., A. Pulcherie Pierre, R. E. Phipps, Dr. F. Matthew Simmonds, William Grell, C. S. René, and H. Sylvester Williams. These comprised the deputation to the MPs in the conference room of Westminster Hall of the House of Commons. A report, probably by Williams, put the number of MPs present at 150 but the *Daily News* gave the names of only twenty-two of those who attended, among them Leonard Courtney, who presided, Sir Charles Dilke, Sir Wilfrid Lawson, Sir W. Kay-Shuttleworth, and Philip Stanhope. Other MPs who were interested would have been attracted by an announcement in *The Times* that some Liberal MPs were to receive, under the auspices of the Cobden Society, a deputation of West Indians on the welfare of the islands, which was being sacrificed to the interests of the sugar planters. The *Daily News* described the deputation as "all natives of Trinidad and men of education, some creoles, and the rest colored gentlemen."[41]

Williams was to claim that he was the "first black man" to speak beneath the roof of the House of Commons. [42] He spoke after Hamel-Smith, Senior, a white Trinidadian who had settled in England but had continued to have business intercourse with the island as a merchant. Williams said the sugar interests in the West Indies had always been voiced in England, but so far as he knew not once had the people's case been put forward. He had sprung from the people, knew their needs, and could testify that they were distressed. The sole cause of the depression in the West Indies, he asserted, was the sugar monopoly, which the laws supported. As on other occasions, he insisted that the blacks were not lazy; they would work and prosper if they were not systematically discouraged. They asked for a vote in their own government and with that they would know how to remove their difficulties. They spoke, he said, as patriotic British citizens claiming their rights. In reply to the questions of the MPs, Williams explained that the people of Trinidad had not formally appointed the deputation; he knew their needs from contact with them and from the island newspapers.[43] Alcazar, one of the deputation, complained later of the newspaper reports; both Hamel-Smith and Williams had made lengthy speeches but "scanty justice" had been done to the "oratory of the occasion."

Chamberlain referred to the deputation in a statement at question time in the House of Commons in reply to Sir Charles Dilke. Predictably he declared that it was "absolutely impossible" to give representative government to the West Indies and "perfectly absurd" to give household suffrage to "the Negro population" because they would not value it.

Despite the merit of the case and his skill in advocating it, Williams's campaign for constitutional reform in Trinidad could not have succeeded in an era of high imperialism and with arch-imperialist Chamberlain as colonial secretary. And although Williams continued to maintain an interest in Trinidad affairs, increasingly he turned his attention to Africa.

NOTES

1. The word seems to have been first used by T. Thomas Fortune, editor of the *New York Age,* in preference to "Negro." West Indian Rev. Dr. W. B. Derrick said editor Fortune had "discovered and popularized the word." *New York Age,* October 23, 1891. See also *New Age* (London), February 3, 1898.

2. See Emma Lou Thornbrugh, *Timothy Thomas Fortune: Militant Journalist* (Chicago: University of Chicago Press, 1972).

3. *New York Age,* 1891, passim.

4. Ibid., March 22, 1906.

5. Edwin S. Redkey, *Black Exodus* (New Haven: Yale University Press, 1969), passim; see also Hollis R. Lynch, *Edward Wilmot Blyden, Pan-Negro Patriot, 1832-1912* (London and New York: Oxford University Press, 1967), chap. 6.

6. *New York Age,* October 3, 1891.

7. Ibid., October 10, 1891.

8. Ibid., October 3, 1891.

9. Ibid.

10. Registrar, Dalhousie University, to the author, February 20, 1968.

11. Emerson Biggar, *Canada, A Memorial Volume* (London: E. Stanford, 1889), p. 31.

12. Registrar, Dalhousie University, to the author.

13. Robin W. Winks, *The Blacks in Canada: A History* (New Haven: Yale University Press, 1971), chap. 1.

14. *Marylebone Mercury,* November 17, 1906.

15. Registrar, University of London King's College, to the author, June 26, 1968.

16. *Marylebone Mercury* and *West London Gazette,* November 17, 1906.

17. Walpole to Buxton, May 13, 1902, Anti-Slavery Papers, Rhodes House Library, Oxford.

18. *Review of Reviews* (January 1897): 4.

19. Ibid. (August 1896):43.

20. Ibid. (November 1897): 370. "Sjambokking" is flogging with a rhinoceros-hide whip.

21. Ibid.

22. *Times,* January 20, 1897.

23. James L. Garvin, *Life of Joseph Chamberlain* (London: Macmillan, 1934), 3: 185n.

24. *New Age,* June 3, 1897.

25. *Port-of-Spain Gazette,* June 25, 1897.

26. H. S. Williams, "Trinidad, B.W.I.," in *British America,* vol. 3, British Empire Series (London: Kegan Paul, 1900), p. 464.

27. *Port-of-Spain Gazette,* June 27, 1897.

28. Librarian, Gray's Inn, to the author, December 5, 1966. Gray's Inn is one of the four Inns of Court, ancient societies of advocates that set the standards of education and conduct for the English bar and exercise disciplinary powers over its members.

29. *The Times,* April 30, 1898.

30. Ibid., June 8, 1898.

31. *Port-of-Spain Gazette,* June 2, 1901.

32. Envelope enclosing letter from Williams to "Miss Powell," December 20, 1897, Williams Papers, Barataria, Trinidad.

33. *Rochester, Chatham and Gillingham Journal,* April 25, 1904.

34. Williams to Agnes Powell, December 20, 1897, Williams Papers, Barataria, Trinidad.

35. *New Age,* January 20, 1898.

36. Conversations with Mr. H. F. Sylvester Williams in Trinidad, November 1968.

37. Prefatory note to British Empire Series by William Sheowring, honorary secretary, Institute Committee. From internal evidence Williams's lecture, "Trinidad, B.W.I.," would have been delivered after the diamond jubilee in 1897.

38. Williams, "Trinidad, B.W.I.," p. 474.

39. The pamphlet is not extant. Its text was published in the *Mirror,* April 6, 1899.

40. Ibid.

41. *Port-of-Spain Gazette,* April 6, 1899.

42. *Mirror,* July 8, 1901.

43. *Port-of-Spain Gazette,* April 6, 1899.

"Light and Liberty": 4
The African Association

Williams seems to have found his feet very quickly after he arrived in England in 1896. He immediately perceived a need for a "body of Africans in England representing native opinion in national matters affecting the destiny of the African race." To fill this need, he founded the African Association on September 24, 1897 and was its honorary secretary.[1] The stated purposes of the association were

> to encourage a feeling of unity and to facilitate friendly inter-course among Africans in general; to promote and protect the in-terests of all subjects claiming African descent, wholly or in part, in British colonies and other places, especially in Africa, by circulating accurate information on all subjects affecting their rights and privileges as subjects of the British Empire, by direct appeals to the Imperial and local Governments.[2]

As a result of the activities of the African Association and under its aegis a call was issued as early as 1898 for the 1900 conference in London that first gave currency to the concept of Pan-Africanism. In Fact Williams had conceived of the idea of a world conference of black people in 1897, even before the formation of the African Association.[3]

British rule had inculcated in its colonial subjects an unquestioning faith in the fairness of Britain and the beneficence of Queen Victoria. The British imperial propaganda deceived even sophisticated men. The great Gandhi, writing with evident remorse some years after having formed an Indian ambulance corps to help the British in the "Zulu 'Rebellion,' " said he had believed at the time that the British empire existed for the welfare of the world.[4] And even the distinguished Afro-

American leader, Dr. W. E. B. Du Bois, confessed to having admired Victoria in his youth as a "magnificent symbol of Empire" and seen England, with its flag draped around the world, leading nonwhite peoples to Christian baptism, civilization, and eventual self-rule.[5]

Like so many colonials, Williams was afflicted with the euphoria of the time. They believed the British empire was a blessing to the world and to Africans, though their lands were being filched while they were being brought "the light of civilization." There were times though when Williams had doubts. A chance meeting with an African woman from Natal during a visit to Birmingham on temperance business aroused in Williams a passionate interest in conditions among the Africans in southern Africa. The woman, Mrs. E. V. Kinloch, was the wife of a Scottish engineer in the diamond fields, for there had been interracial marriages in the South African colonies. Mrs. Kinloch was well acquainted with the conditions under which Africans labored in the mines and compounds in which they were herded. So moved was Williams by her account that he persuaded her to speak at a large meeting he was to address. Williams was very pleased with the performance of a "a woman of our race." With his encouragement, Mrs. Kinloch subsequently spoke throughout the country about the plight of blacks in southern Africa.[6] She also received some support from the Women's Temperance Association [7] and the Aborigines Protection Society. [8]

It is possible that Mrs. Kinloch was the "lady, a native of South Africa now lecturing in this country," who complained to the editor of *New Age,* with which the African Association had established some affinity, that it was "astounding" that as soon as she was critical of missionaries, "people here do not like it." She acknowledged that there were some good missionaries abroad but these were "very few." And it may have been Williams who promoted the meeting in York that backed the "Lady's" charge that some missionaries abroad "illtreat my people." The meeting called for exposing the cruel treatment Africans received at the hands of British missionaries.[9]

Williams himself described the compound system as "unchristian, degrading and illegal" and a "blot upon Christian England." In 1901 he told a Trinidad audience that southern Africans were induced to work on contract for British companies, which lodged them in enclosed compounds without their wives for three months at a miserable wage of twopence a day. If they arrived at work two minutes late they were flogged, and at the end of their time they were drugged to find out whether they had swallowed any diamonds. [10]

There was apparently a steady campaign by humanitarian interests against conditions in South Africa, in which Williams and Mrs. Kinloch joined in the months before the formation of the African Association. [11] The Aborigines Protection Society and the British and Foreign Anti-Slavery Society were the two humanitarian organizations of long standing particularly concerned with the inhumane treatment of indigenous peoples, especially in Africa. H. R. Fox-Bourne, the secretary of the Aborigines Protection Society, was to become an honorary member of the African Association. Activities of the humanitarians were regularly reported in the penny weekly *New Age,* which Williams and his friends in the African Association read. Toward the end of August the *New Age* reported that the African "rebels" who had submitted in Bechuanaland were "being marched down to Capetown and hired out to farmers at ten shillings a month." If this was not slavery, *New Age* asked, what was? [12] Williams described these "prisoners" of the Matabele war as "these poor unfortunate people" who had been consigned to Capetown by the Chartered Company and sold "at the stake" as in the "old days of slavery in the United States." According to him, this "so incensed the British public that meetings were held on every hand" and Mrs. Kinloch "went throughout the country" speaking on behalf of those people. [13]

Williams and his friends, aroused, made representations to the British government.[14] It was at this stage apparently that they decided to resort to organized action of their own. They reasoned that if English people so interested themselves in protecting those who were not their kith and kin, why should not they, young men and women of African descent from the West Indies, form an organization to speak for those who were unable to speak for themselves. Williams later urged that Africans unite to do for themselves what he believed no others could do for them, no matter how noble their intentions might be. [15] He told an interviewer in Trinidad that the promoters of the African Association conceived it to be their duty to support the Aborigines Protection Society and the Anti-Slavery Society in their work in order to show the English people that West Indians of African descent were seriously interested in the welfare of their people in Africa. [16]

Among Williams's friends who shared his concern and joined him
in the African Association was Frederick Ellis Bass. [17] Born in
Antigua, Bass had come to Britain after graduating in medicine at
Meharry Medical College in Nashville, Tennessee, to obtain an English
qualification, enabling him to practice in Trinidad where his parents
had migrated from Antigua. Another was the Rev. Henry Mason
Joseph, also from Antigua, who was elected president of the association.
Joseph presided over what was probably the first social gathering of
the members and friends of the African Association on January 11,
1898, at which Williams and Fletcher, the editor of *New Age,* were
among the speakers. It was held at Exeter Hall, the old home of the
abolitionists, then held under lease by George Williams, the founder
of the Young Men's Christian Association, as the YMCA headquarters.
New Age's report of the gathering gave a list of some twenty-eight
persons who were among "many others" present. Apart from Williams,
Joseph, and Fletcher, it lists Mrs. and Miss Joseph, Dr. and Mrs. W.
Law, Mrs. Sivebright Green, Mrs. M. T. Cole, Mr. Harry Gurney, Mr.
F. W. Fox, Mr., Mrs., and Miss T. Bowden Green, Mr. Philip, Mr.
E. A. Durham, Miss Groom, the Misses Powell, Rev. C. W. Farquhar,
Dr. F. Ellis Bass, Dr. E. James Hayford, Mr. Evans, Mr. A. C. Durham,
Mr. R. E. Phipps, and Mr. and Mrs. C. H. Allen.

New Age described Joseph's address of welcome, explaining the
"motives and character" of the association as "remarkably interesting."
It summarized Fletcher's and Mrs. Law's speeches, saying they were
"emphatic on the desirability of the institution and conveyed the impression that if its work is efficiently carried out it would equal in importance that of the Indian National Congress." Rev. C. W. Farquhar of
Isles de Los, West Africa, gave "an able and eloquent" address, "The
Future of the Race." A vote of thanks to the president was moved by
Dr. Hayford of Gold Coast, West Africa, and seconded by Williams
who said the members desired the association to be as representative
as possible so that information should be "direct and first hand" from
various parts of the empire. [18] He suggested that branches should be encouraged in the colonies and protectorates. [19]

It is possible now to identify only a few of those who attended the
function. The Durham brothers came from Trinidad and were the sons
of George Horatio Durham, a retired schoolmaster turned cocoa planter
and merchant. Ernest became a barrister as did his brother Frederick,

who wrote *The Lone Star of Liberia* (a defense of that black republic published in 1892) just before he was called up to the bar by Lincoln's Inn at the age of 22. Little is known of their brother A. C. Durham, except that he was assistant secretary of the African Association.[20] Rev. C. W. Farquhar, an Antiguan, was a former master at the Mico School at St. John's Antigua. He had served there fifteen years when he was ordained deacon in the Church of England and arrived at the Island of Cassa (Isles de Los), West Africa, in October 1890 to organize a boys' boarding school there for the Rio Pongo Mission.[21] Richard E. Phipps, like Williams from Arouca, Trinidad, was also reading for the bar.

The only African-born identified was Dr. Hayford, one of the Hayford brothers of the Gold Coast, but there may have been other Africans in the gathering. Among the English friends only some are identifiable. Henry Gurney was a member of the committee of the Aborigines Protection Society and an early honorary member of the African Association. Mr. and Mrs. Allen were probably the Charles H. Allens, Mr. Allen being the honorary secretary of the British and Foreign Anti-Slavery Society. In addition to Gurney and Fox-Bourne, other Aborigines Protection Society members who were honorary members of the association were Philip Stanhope, MP, and George W. E. Russell, MP, [22] a prolific writer and one of the leading figures of the Liberal Forwards movement, which spearheaded the revival of the Liberal party.

In publicizing a pamphlet containing the rules, aims, and objectives of the African Association, the organ of the Anti-Slavery Society wrote it was "pleased to give our hearty good wishes to this newly formed body." It added that persons wishing information about the association might address Mr. H. S. Williams at Gray's Inn.[23] According to the pamphlet, the association had been organized because there was no "body of Africans" in England representing "native opinion in national matters affecting the destiny of the African race." It aimed at encouraging unity so as to facilitate friendly intercourse among "Africans in general." It planned to promote and protect the interests of all "subjects" claiming African descent, wholly or in part, "in British colonies and other places." Its scope was confined to British subjects, and it proposed to protect their rights "by appealing to British and the colonial governments to redress their wrongs." [24]

Good wishes for the association were not universal. "Certain English

persons" gave the association but three months to live. They could not
see colored people uniting for such a purpose. Williams had confidently
insisted that the association would act on its own, draft its own rules,
and not be led by Europeans.[25] The association survived for four years,
though there were times when the prediction about a short life span
nearly came true.

In keeping with the association's pledge to protect the interests of
"our African brethren," Williams contacted well-disposed MPs to ask
questions about colonial conditions, particularly in South Africa. He
wrote Joseph Chamberlain, colonial secretary, about the welfare of
Africans in Rhodesia[26] and to the newspapers on behalf of the
association. A letter he wrote that was published in the *Leader* about
this time was an appeal from a member of "the African race . . . to my
white brothers who read the *Leader* on behalf of my ill-treated countrymen."[27] Although he was not African-born, he identified himself with
Africans, possibly because most English people did not differentiate
among people with black skins.

In justifying his role as their leader, Williams explained that the
grievances of the British people were easily redressed; they had the
right to elect representatives to Parliament while the "native races,"
the "nominally British subjects," were not allowed their full rights.
He condemned this as manifestly unfair and questioned the methods
used under the pretext of civilizing blacks and the motives of the
"civilizers" who gave them an "adulterated 'Christianity.' " He
charged the British government with condoning the introduction of
slavery in South Africa under the leadership of Cecil Rhodes. British
policy had left a blot on the "broad escutcheon of the nation's
standard," which could be erased only by public opinion. He appealed
to the nation on behalf of the African Association to call upon its
representatives to ensure fairness and justice to blacks. He wrote that
the Association would welcome "the agencies of a high civilization"
(for example, the industrial schools and the basic teachings of Christ)
that would provide education and a moral structure. Williams did
not advocate a complete westernization of the African. Nothing was
to be forced upon him, and he was to adopt only what was good in the
European while retaining the best of his own culture.

There is a certain naiveté in Williams's faith in the power of
English public opinion and his confidence that it could be persuaded

to seek a reversal of policies that expanded Britain's power and influence even though bringing suffering to millions of the African people. The pioneer economist of imperialism, J. A. Hobson, writes of "the direct and conscious work of politicians and their organizations" in influencing public opinion at this time. Prominent among these was the South African League with its emissaries active both in South Africa and in England, "ably seconding the efforts of Mr. Rhodes' press." Rhodes was president of the league, and he and other leading capitalists provided its financial support. The league's efforts were directed at involving imperial power in South Africa, and it was able to "impress the mind of the High Commissioner (Lord Milner) and to secure his authoritative approval of every possible technicality which they might employ to influence the British Government."[28] With such a colossus in the field the puny and fragile African Association had a most formidable competitor for the public mind, but Williams had bigger plans to attract attention in the hope of winning sympathy for his cause.

The question has been raised why the conveners of the Pan-African Conference chose the year 1900, and the answer has been offered that perhaps it was because it marked the beginning of a new century. There is, however, no evidence that this was taken into consideration; rather, they acted on more practical grounds. Williams, it will be recalled, had conceived the idea of a world conference of blacks well before formation of the African Association.[29] He and his friends realized that it would be difficult to get people to come to London just for a conference, even one so potentially important. If there were some other important event to bring them to London in sufficient numbers they might be induced to attend a gathering of "representatives of the race" held about the same time. Queen Victoria's diamond jubilee in 1897 had brought many of them to London, and while the magnificent outpouring of loyalty coincided with the agitation against the ill-treatment of the Matabele, the collapse of the sugar industry in the West Indies, and famine and cholera in India, the African Association had not then been formed. Even at that time there had been widespread publicity for the great exposition the French were planning to open in Paris in April 1900. Such an occasion might attract many blacks, and those who were going to Paris might be induced to combine their trip with a visit to London for a meeting about Africa and Africans. And so it did.

The first steps were taken at a meeting of the association on March 19, 1898. Those attending decided to issue a circular announcing the intention "to hold a conference in the month of May, 1900, in order to take steps to influence public opinion in existing proceedings and conditions affecting the welfare of the natives of the various parts of the British Empire, viz., South Africa, West Africa and the British West Indies."[30] Attention was being concentrated on conditions in those lands under British rule, for in London the spotlight was focussed on the conditions for which the British government was responsible and for which it was answerable to Parliament.

Williams and H. Mason Joseph, president of the association, must have been happy indeed to meet Benito Sylvain in December 1897 when he visited London on his way back to Paris from a journey home to Haiti.[31] Sylvain, only twenty-nine and a year older than Williams (whom he described as "a young student"), had already had a crowded career as a man of affairs. He had gone to Paris when he was only seventeen and became a naval trainee. At nineteen, blocked by a decree barring foreigners from entry into the French naval school, he had turned from science to letters and, after a short period of study, obtained the Bachelor of Philosophy degree. At twenty his articles defending his race from the attacks of Gaston Jollivet in Le Matin "caused a sensation" in Paris. Then, after a period in Journalism in Haiti, he entered his country's diplomatic service, serving in 1889 as secretary at the London legation. But he was back in Paris the following year when he refuted the hostile articles of Charles Canivet and others whom he categorized as "aristocrats of the skin."[32] In August 1890 he had launched his own journal, La Fraternité, dedicated to the interests of his country and his race[33] and formed a students' organization, the Association of Black Youth of Paris (L'Association de la jeunesse noire de Paris).[34] Inspired by Cardinal Lavigerie's campaign against African slavery, he had taken an active part in 1890 and 1891 as Haitian representative in the Anti-Slavery Congresses in Paris and Brussels.

It must have interested Williams and Joseph still more that Sylvain had been on a diplomatic mission for his president to the court of the

Emperor Menelik of Abyssinia. They discussed with him the idea of a conference on the welfare of the race, and there must have been mutual surprise at the near identity of their thoughts. In early 1895, Sylvain, deeply concerned about the position of blacks and the scorn with which the white world regarded them, had sought the advice of a fellow countryman, Anténor Firmin, Haitian minister to France, on the idea of a world ethnological congress as part of the Paris Universal Exposition in 1900. Firmin, while foreign minister in 1891, had won renown for Haiti's victory in a diplomatic battle with the United States, which was pressing for a lease of the Môle St. Nicolas on its northern coast for a naval and coaling station. [35] He was also the author of *De l'Egalité des Races Humaines* (1885) [On the equality of the human races], countering Count Arthur de Gobineau's *Essai sur l'Inégalité des Races Humaines* (1853-1855). (Gobineau theorized that racial composition was a determining factor in the development of civilization and that white societies flourished best when not contaminated by other racial strains, which inhibited creativity and ensured corruption and immorality.) Firmin was to be made vice-president for Haiti of the Pan-African Association. The ethnological congress Sylvain proposed and Firmin supported would have brought together learned men and spokesmen of the African race to discuss and settle finally the question of inferior and superior races. As he saw it, the congress would be an appeal to modern science, which he considered "more impartial and better informed" than the old science, which, to salve the conscience of a slave-owning Europe, had proclaimed the innate inferiority of blacks. [36] This grandiose idea for an ethnological conference had been rendered abortive by Haitian internal conditions. After his discussions with Williams and Joseph, Sylvain agreed that instead of the ethnological congress they should call a meeting of delegates from the people of African descent with European learned men, philanthropists, and politicians. [37]

The original scope of the conference was later enlarged, apparently as the result of a meeting of a number of blacks from both sides of the Atlantic who were in London on other business. The conference originally had been designed to combat "the widespread ignorance which is prevalent in England about the treatment of the Native Races under British rule." [38] This was enlarged to cover "the treatment of native races under European and American rule," and specifically those

in "South Africa, West Africa, West Indies and United States of
America."[39]

The conference date, originally scheduled for May 1900 with the
Paris exposition in mind, was changed on the advice of a number of
"leading men" of the race from Africa, the United States, and the West
Indies who, while visiting London for various reasons, attended a preparatory meeting of the Pan-African Conference committee on June 12,
1899. They considered July more suitable, and the committee agreed
that the dates should be July 23, 24, and 25, bearing in mind that the
World's Christian Endeavor Convention would be opening at the Alex-
andra Palace, London, on July 16. [40] Indeed some of the clerical in-
invitees to the Pan-African Conference may have indicated they would be
coming to London after May to attend the convention. The official
report of the conference tells of these "leading men" having "rendered
valuable service," evidently by their advice to the committee. They
would also have given publicity to the proposed conference on their
return home, and some of them were listed in the report as branch
officers of the Pan-African Association founded at the conference.
These advisers, some of whose names are given in the conference report, constitute a galaxy of remarkable men who, had they been able
to attend the conference as they intended, would have added considerably to its dramatic impact. The report gives the names of Bishop
James T. Holly, Bishop James Johnson, Bishop Henry McNeal Turner,
the Rev. Dr. Majola Agbebi, the Rev. C. W. Farquhar, Judge David
Augustus Straker, Professor W. S. Scarborough, Henry Richard
Cargill, J. Tengo Jabavu, J. Otonba Payne, and Professor Booker T.
Washington. [41]

Though some of them might not yet have reached the peak of their
careers, they were certainly among the leading blacks of the day. Professor Washington, while well known, had not yet gained fame as "the
sage of Tuskegee" though he had already attained a position of power
and leadership among his people in the wake of the famous Atlanta
compromise speech of 1895. In London Washington gave a public
address on the "condition and prospects of the colored races in
America."[42]

Bishop Holly of the Episcopal church in Haiti, where he had
settled, had been joint promoter with Martin R. Delany of an emigration convention in Cleveland, Ohio, in August 1854. His ideas differed

from those of his fellow emigrationists; they were for settlement in Central America at one time and in Africa at another, while he supported emigration from the United States to Haiti, in which he received the backing of the Haitian government.

Bishop Johnson, a friend of Edward Blyden, who was thinking in terms of Pan-African before the term was coined, was born in Sierra Leone of recaptive parents. He led the agitation for an African church but stopped short of leaving the Anglican church when it was time for the new church to be established. He was a missionary in Sierra Leone, Lagos, Yorubaland, and the Lower Niger Delta. In London on February, 18, 1900, he was consecrated an assistant bishop of the Niger Delta. [43]

Bishop Turner was a militant leader of the African Methodist Episcopal church and, since the 1870s, had been a champion of migration to Africa. He was responsible for the spread of the influence of his church in South Africa. Agbebi (formerly David B. Vincent) was a Baptist minister, headmaster of Hope School, Lagos, which catered to children of the poor, and whom Edward Wilmot Blyden, in 1902, described as the embodiment of the "African personality." [44] He championed the retention of African customs and institutions not offensive to humanity. An advocate of an independent nondenominational African church, he was the main force in the establishment of the Independent Baptist Church in Lagos. Farquhar, a West Indian missionary in West Africa, had attended the January 1898 social gathering of the African Association at Exeter Hall. Judge Straker, who apparently had retired from a judgeship in Michigan, had three publications to his credit, including a small work on the life and times of Toussaint L'Ouverture. Professor Scarborough was a distinguished classical scholar who became president of Wilberforce University, Ohio. Henry Richard Cargill was a Jamaican planter, merchant, and politician of Port Antonio, described as "an ardent member of the Baptist Church." [45] Jabavu, a South African and a product of the Lovedale Mission, was editor of the African weekly, *Imvo Zabantsundu* [African Opinion], in King Williams Town, Cape Colony, and influential in South African politics before the Africans were disfranchised. Otunba Payne was chief registrar of Lagos, chairman of the board of Hope School, and host of Blyden and a member of the committee which invited him to pay his first visit to Lagos in December 1890.

The meeting of these men of African descent, of varying backgrounds, and from scattered lands is indicative of their common interest in the destiny of their oppressed brethren and their readiness to make common cause in an effort to protect and uplift them. Another significant fact is the predominance of the missionary element among them. The term "Pan-African" was not applied to their meeting though it was used before the 1900 conference with reference to its preparatory committee.

The oldest document in which the term "Pan-African" is found is a letter dated November 11, 1899, written by Williams to J. M. Bourne, a member of the African Association who had written on November 4 apparently protesting that the convening of a "Pan African Conference"— Williams wrote it without the hyphen—was a departure from the constitution of the association. Williams, after consultation with Joseph, denied this. Apparently Bourne's was an angry letter for Williams replied that they regretted its tone and failed to see the cause of his "summary request,"perhaps indicating that Bourne had demanded that the plans be cancelled. Williams insisted that there had been no deviation and that in fact they meant to adhere to the principles laid down. Williams suggested that perhaps Bourne might not have taken into account circulars dealing with the "more effective execution" of the work of the association. A "Pan African Conference," he argued, would bring the leaders of the people in greater sympathy with the movement. Besides, replies received so far had been quite favorable, and they were hopeful of the conference's success. [46]

Bourne probably was not an original member of the association; had he been, he would have known that the idea of a conference had been present from the beginning and that a formal decision to call one had been taken at a meeting of March 18, 1898.

Williams evidently felt it was time for the African people to be fighting their own battles, and he was tired of being asked by paternal though sympathetic liberals, "What are the natives doing in the struggle to secure their own rights?"

In naming the conference, Williams and his group must have been aware of the pan-Slav movement, the oldest of the "pan-" movements, which had held a demonstration in Prague in 1898. Then too there was the pan-Germanic movement represented by the "Alldeutsche Verband," which, also in the same year, had held a conference in Munich attended by delegates from every part of Germany and from local groups that had been established among German settlers abroad. The "Verband" sought to stimulate the patriotism of race, to emphasize the solidarity of all German-speaking peoples, and to prepare the way for their political union.[47]

The establishment of the three German colonies in Africa with a total area of 825,000 square miles was a source of possible conflict between the pan-Germans and the pan-Africanists. The pan-German propaganda so disturbed the Austrian government that it banned their publications. The pan-Africanists were constrained to be more moderate by the very circumstances of their race. Unlike the German-speaking peoples, who were largely concentrated in a land mass in adjoining countries and had a common language, the Africans were scattered widely over two continents divided by a vast ocean, had no common language, and were dominated by different white nations. Shorn of their cultural identity and out of a necessity to survive and progress, they had adopted the ways of life and thought—the languages, religions, moral code, and the dress—of their European enslavers. They were now asking whether this had been right.

It is not known whether any English members other than Bourne objected to the Pan-African Conference, but his challenge shows that from the beginning the idea gave rise to controversy among the membership. Possibly Bourne sensed that the African Association was headed for a political turn that was too revolutionary for him to contemplate. But Williams and his friends, while appreciating and not rejecting the help of white friends, were convinced that Africans were able to and should protect their own interests themselves.

The task of organizing the conference was entrusted to the Pan-African Conference committee, which immediately began sounding out possible participants. It chose the motto "Light and Liberty." Williams was listed on the letterhead as general secretary, with the following other officers: chairman, Rev. H. Mason Joseph, M.A.; vice-chairman, Rev. Thos. L. Johnson; secretary for West Indies, R. E. Phipps; and secretary for West Africa, Henry Plange. [48] There was provision for a secretary for South Africa but none was named on the letterhead. The treasurer was Henry Macpherson, who has not been identified.

No more is heard of him, but his name appeared in the list of contributors to the funds. Plange evidently was from West Africa and so was
Johnson.

The first order of business was to collect money to finance the conference, but only two gifts were received during 1899—five pounds from
J. Thompson and four pounds from D. Campbell, whose identities are
unknown. [49] By the beginning of April 1900, Williams was able to report that two delegates had arrived for the conference to be held in
July. The first to arrive was John E. Quinlan, sworn land surveyor, of
St. Lucia, West Indies. The next was Reverend S. R. B. Solomon of
Accra, West Africa, whose name does not appear in any list of participants in the conference. [50] Quinlan had made the novel claim in
a memorandum to the West India Royal Commission of 1897 that
the British Parliament should compensate the descendants of the
slaves. But he said that they were asking for a loan instead of the "free
gift to which we are justly entitled."[51] At the end of May, Williams had
received letters from South Africa and the United States of America
from "many invitees" who had said they would be arriving in June or
July. He appealed for help from the Anti-Slavery Society "in making the
occasion memorable,"[52] but no help was given despite the fact that the
society's organ had expressed good wishes to the African Association
two years earlier and had later publicized the proposed conference.
Perhaps the humanitarians found a world conference of blacks too
frightening a project as the time got nearer for the delegates to meet.

Lack of support from the Anti-Slavery Society did not daunt Williams
and his supporters. The arrangements were well in hand, and funds were
coming. They had timed the conference for the convenience of those
who were also attending the Universal Paris Exposition and the World
Christian Endeavor Convention in London. It might not have been
possible otherwise for more than a few of them to come the long
way to London just for the Pan-African Conference. For instance,
Dr. Du Bois had to travel steerage from New York to Paris where he
was preparing part of the American Negro exhibit at the exposition.[53]

For the band of young West Indians and Africans promoting the
conference, it was a grand adventure. With an eye to dramatizing their
world conclave of Africans and people of African descent, at Williams's
suggestion, they decided to ask the bishop of London, the scholarly Dr.
Mandell Creighton, to open the conference.[54]

The first function in connection with the conference took place sixteen days before it was to open. The liberal New Reform Club gave an "at home" in which the principal guests were "the delegates appointed to attend the Pan-African Conference which is held in London this month for the purpose of declaring native opinion upon matters affecting the aboriginal races in various parts of the world." [55] In reporting the meeting, the press used the term "Pan-African" for the first time.

A meeting was held at the end of the function under the presidency of the honorary treasurer of the club, P. W. Clayden, who had been secretary of the Liberal Forwards movement. Williams declared that the conference would be the first occasion upon which black men would assemble in England to speak for themselves and endeavor to influence public opinion in their favor. It would consider the position of blacks in South Africa; they must see to it that their interests were not overlooked in any settlement effected following the South African war. [56] Other speakers were Quinlan, Mrs. Cobden Unwin, wife of the publisher T. Fisher Unwin and daughter of the great Radical politician Richard Cobden, and Dr. R. F. Colenso, who had been with his father, the famous bishop of Natal who had carried on a harassing and wearing warfare against ill-treatment of the indigenous people of South Africa.

At a meeting of the African Association a week before the conference opened, an engrossed memorial was presented to Bishop James Johnson on his leaving for Lagos to assume the assistant bishopric of the Lower Niger. It may not have been known to all those honoring him that "Holy" Johnson had twice before refused the bishopric and that in his appointment he was being denied the full authority of the office and he was only, as was said, "half a bishop." [57] They knew of him as West Africa's most prominent African clergyman who, in earlier days in Sierra Leone, stimulated by his friend Edward Wilmot Blyden, had been a leading agitator for an African church and later a temperate but forthright legislator, having been appointed to the legislative council of Lagos by Governor Cornelius Alfred Moloney.

While the memorialists thought it fit to pay "an humble tribute" to the bishop's personal qualities and achievements, they used the address to declare their belief that it was time for blacks to develop their own "talent and energy." They acknowledged that by a "cruel design" the race had been denied its share in the progress of the world and its "great men" allowed little scope for the development of their powers and capacity, but they found consolation and encouragement in the growing *esprit de corps*.

They admitted that the position of the African—"either at home or under the flags of the known powers"—was not "too reassuring." They believed firmly that their efforts should be directed to the education of the young so as to bring forth the "prolific possibilities of the race," that they should develop "our own chroniclers," and that the members of the race should institute and support "our own libraries and organizations." Thus, they would be able to march side by side with "our more fortunate Caucasian brothers." [58] They were conscious of the distortions of history as presented by Caucasians and of the need for the balance to be redressed.

The partial list of signatories to the memorial includes the names of some of the delegates who had arrived for the conference and of resident members of the African Association. It is recorded as follows:

F. E. R. Johnson, Ex-Attorney General, Liberia;
Benito Sylvain, Aide-de-Camp to the Emperor Menelik, Abyssinia
Henry F. Downing, Ex- U.S.A. Consul, Loanda.
Mrs. M. T. Cole, A. R. Hamilton (Jamaica), N. W. Holm, R. E. Phipps,
A. P. Pierre, M. F. Ribeiro, Dr. Schomerus, D. E. Tobias, J. W. D.
Worrell, H. Sylvester Williams (Hon. Sec.) and others.[59]

Bishop Johnson expressed regret that he could not stay and attend "the first and unique" gathering of his kinsmen from all parts of the globe. He praised Williams's zeal and energy, and he thought it encouraging that nearly all concerned in this "wonderful" movement were young men from the West Indies, the United States of America, Liberia, and Abyssinia—determined to press the cause of the race to a successful issue. Urging his audience to have confidence and faith in one another, Bishop Johnson declared that "the Pan-African Association is the beginning of a union I had long hoped for, and would to God it could be universal!" [60]

With these words of encouragement from a distinguished kinsman, the first pan-Africanists were ready to begin their task to take "Light and Liberty" to others of their race everywhere.

NOTES

1. *Lagos Standard,* July 27, 1898; see also *Gold Coast Chronicle,* August 12, 1898.

2. *Report of the Pan-African Conference* (London: The Pan-African Association, 1900).

3. Ibid.

4. M. K. Gandhi, *Autobiography: Story of My Experiments with Truth* (Washington: Public Affairs Press, 1954), p. 313.

5. W. E. B. Du Bois, *Dusk of Dawn* (New York: Schocken Books, 1940; reprint ed., 1968), p. 41.

6. *Mirror,* June 1, 1901.

7. Kathleen Fitzpatrick, *Lady Henry Somerset* (Boston: Little, Brown, 1923), p. 120.

8. *Mirror,* June 1, 1901.

9. *New Age,* May 27, 1897.

10. *Mirror,* June 1, 1901.

11. Ibid.

12. *New Age,* September 2, 1897.

13. *Mirror,* June 1, 1901.

14. Ibid.

15. Ibid.

16. Ibid., May 17, 1901.

17. Ibid., June 1, 1901.

18. Ernest James Hayford, 1858-1913, a medical doctor, was the brother of J. E. Casely Hayford, 1864-1930, prominent Gold Coast lawyer and author and the leading West African nationalist of his time.

19. *New Age,* January 20, 1898.

20. *Creole Bitters* (May 1901).

21. A. H. Barrow, *Fifty Years in Western Africa* (London: SPCK, 1900), pp. 131, 135.

22. *Anti-Slavery Reporter* (March-May 1899): 112.

23. Ibid. (July-August 1898): 182.

24. Ibid.; see also *Report of the Pan-African Conference, 1900,* p. 1.

25. *Mirror,* June 1, 1901.

26. Imanuel Geiss, *Panafrikanismus* (Frankfurt am Main: Europaische Verlagsanstalt, 1965), p. 382, quoting *Lagos Standard,* January 4, 1899.

27. Undated clipping from *Leader,* letter headed "An African's Appeal," Williams papers, Barataria, Trinidad.

28. J. A. Hobson, *Psychology of Jingoism* (London: J. Richards, 1901), pp. 136-37.

29. *Report of the Pan-African Conference, 1900*, p. 1.

30. Ibid., p. 2; Anti-Slavery Reporter, March-May 1899, p. 112.

31. Benito Sylvain, *Du Sort des Indigènes dans les Colonies d'Exploitation* (Paris: Boyer, 1901), p. 508.

32. Benito Sylvain, "L Évolution de la Race Noire," in *Les Conferences antiesclavagistes libres* (Brussels: Imprimerie Populaire, 1892), p. 53.

33. Sylvain, *Du Sort des Indigènes*, p. 508.

34. Ibid., p. 509. There is no indication of the countries of origin of the members of this association. Sylvain does not indicate whether it was still in existence in 1900 when his countryman, Jean Price-Mars the ethnologist, was a medical student. Like Sylvain, Price-Mars, was interested in the subject of the equality of races. Léon Damas, "Price-Mars, Father of Haitianism," in *Presénce Africaine* (June-September 1960). The colored Martinique politician, Henry Lémery, who arrived in Paris as a student in 1893 and remained to become a cabinet minister, wrote that Antillians pursuing higher studies at the time were few; see his *D'une République à l'autre: Souvenirs de la Mêlée Politique, 1894-1944* (Paris: La Table Ronde, 1964), p. 11.

35. Frederick Douglass, *Life and Times of Frederick Douglass* (New York: Macmillan, 1962), pp. 596ff. Douglass was minister to Haiti and gives an account of the negotiations conducted by Rear Admiral Gherardi. See also Rayford W. Logan, *Diplomatic Relations of the United States with Haiti, 1776-1891* (Chapel Hill: University of North Carolina Press), 1941.

36. Sylvain, *Du Sort des Indigènes*, pp. 507-8.

37. Ibid., p. 509.

38. *Anti-Slavery Reporter* (March-May 1899): 112.

39. *Report of the Pan-African Conference, 1900*, p. 2.

40. Ibid.

41. Ibid., p. 2.

42. *Times*, July 4, 1899.

43. E. A. Ayandele, *Holy Johnson: Pioneer of African Nationalism* (New York: Humanities Press, 1970), passim.

44. Blyden was a leading pan-African intellectual of his time. See Hollis R. Lynch, *Edward Wilmot Blyden: Pan-Negro Patriot, 1832-1912* (New York: Oxford University Press, 1967), pp. 238-40.

45. *Jamaica Who's Who* (Kingston: Stephen A. Hill, 1916).

46. Williams to Bourne, November 11, 1899, Anti-Slavery Papers, Rhodes House Library, Oxford.

47. *Times,* October 6, 1898.
48. Williams to Buxton, April 2, 1900 Anti-Slavery Papers.
49. *Report of the Pan-African Conference, 1900,* p. 16.
50. Williams to Buxton, April 2, 1900, Anti-Slavery Papers. An early Gold Coast nationalist, the Reverend Mr. Solomon later changed his name to Attoh-Ahuma and authored two books: *Memoirs of West African Celebrities* (Liverpool: D. Marples, 1905) and *The Gold Coast Nation and National Consciousness* (Liverpool: D. Marples, 1911). For an account of his career, see Robert July, *The Origins of Modern African Thought* (New York: Fredrick Praeger, 1968), pp. 341-44.
51. *Report of West India Royal Commission* (London, 1897), 3:74.
52. Williams to Buxton, May 31, 1900, Anti-Slavery Papers.
53. W. E. B. Du Bois, *Autobiography of W. E. B. Du Bois* (New York: International Publishers, 1968), p. 221.
54. *Mirror,* June 1, 1901.
55. *Times,* July 7, 1970.
56. Ibid.
57. E. A. Ayandele, *Holy Johnson: Pioneer of African Nationalism* (New York: Humanities Press, 1970), passim.
58. *Report of the Pan-African Conference, 1900,* p. 3.
59. Ibid., p. 4. Also see "Who Was Who at the Pan-African Conference" in Appendix A to this book where some of the signatories are mentioned. N. W. Holm and Dr. Schomerus are not mentioned elsewhere. Du Bois evidently had not yet arrived, having gone to the Paris exposition, and Bishop Walters was probably busy with the Christian Endeavor Convention.
60. Ibid., pp. 4-5

"Assailing London":   **5**
The 1900 Pan-African
Conference

In the year 1900, when the Pan-African Conference met, imperialism
was at its zenith. During the last twenty years of the nineteenth century,
Great Britain added to its empire Nigeria, Asante, British East Africa
(Kenya), Uganda, Nyasaland, Rhodesia, and Bechuanaland in Africa;
the Sudan, Somaliland, and Zanzibar in the Islamic world; and North
Borneo, Sarawak, Pahang, Kowloon, Wei-hai-wai, and Burma in the Far
East. [1] Britain also had extraterritorial rights in thirty-five Chinese
cities. None of these territories was self-governed.

The military, which were extending the bounds of empire "wider
still and wider," were the heroes of the day and they lorded over the
"lesser breed without the law." This feeling was not confined to the
soldiery, however. The *Times* could say of the news from Peking, where
the Boxers and Chinese troops had besieged the European merchants,
"None of the messages, unfortunately, contains anything to alleviate
materially the profound anxiety all over the *civilized world* for the
Europeans in the capital" (italics added). War was everywhere, and the
British followed its every ebb and flow, whether in South Africa, in
Asante and Nigeria, or in China.

In January 1901, the London journal *West Africa and Traders
Review Illustrated* wrote: "We have had more wars in West Africa since
Mr. Chamberlain went to the Colonial Office than during a generation
before." It was really the culmination of the twofold effect of the widespread acceptance of the doctrine of the survival of the fittest, expressed in the growth of militarism and the cultivation of the ideas of
race superiority and the divine national mission.[2]

Colonials like Williams in London must have been taken aback by
the popular reaction to the relief of besieged Mafeking, which J. A.
Hobson in his *Psychology of Jingoism* described as a "democratic satur-

nalia" generally admitted to be a "revelation of hitherto unknown British character." Thornton described the "flag-waving, drunkenness and maniacal shouting" as "a state of public witlessness that caused a shiver in the most patriotic of (West End) club members." The journalists coined the word "mafficking" to describe the extravagant behavior of the London crowd on that May 17.

An account of the conference by Bishop Alexander Walters appears in his autobiography, *My Life and Work* (1917), and most writers on pan-Africanism have used it as the basis for all their conjectures about the original meaning and aims of the movement. Another delegate, Sylvain, also wrote about the conference, but his work either is not known or, being in French, has been ignored. [3] A brief mention of the conference is also found in the life of Mandell Creighton, the bishop of London, who formally opened it. But Dr. W. E. B. Du Bois, who also participated in the conference, for two decades afterward paid no immediate attention to the conference and its ideas in his prolific writings. Other than a passing mention in 1920 in *Darkwater* and in May 1921 in *The Crisis,* organ of the National Association for the Advancement of Colored People, which he edited, his first published reference to it came forty-six years later in his book, *The World and Africa.* It is this account that is reproduced as Du Bois's contribution to the *History of the Pan-African Congress,* edited by George Padmore. Furthermore, there is no reference either to Williams or to the conference in Du Bois's posthumously published autobiography. In a calendar of his public life appended to the autobiography, the conference merits a one-line mention in connection with an erroneous claim to the secretaryship for Du Bois.

Bishop Walters's report appears faulty in certain particulars though he presided over all the plenary sessions, which were held in Westminster Town Hall on July 23, 24, and 25, 1900. It seems he wrote an account of the conference in 1901 but confessed he had forgotten the names of the branch vice-presidents and secretaries elected at the conference other than those for the United States of America. [4] That account formed the basis of the report of the conference presented in *My Life and Work.* Walters's departure for Europe was delayed because the ship he was booked on burned, and he had to travel to Montreal for another ship. But in Walters's autobiography the ship's burning and his traveling by another ship are placed in 1890, contradicting Walters's own con-

temporary account in the *Colored American.* [5] Walters mentioned the
names of thirty-five representatives though, speaking in Trinidad in
1901, Williams spoke of American representatives "in hundreds." [6]
The other members of the African Association resident in London who
were not delegates probably attended the sessions. Some of the persons
who had attended the Paris Exposition and then come to London
dropped in as curious or interested spectators while viewing the sights
of London. [7] Only Sylvain mentioned Judge Straker of Michigan and a
Miss Adams from Ireland who is also listed among contributors to the
conference fund. [8] Furthermore, Williams mentioned a few names that
do not appear in the Walters list, which itself does not include some of
the names of persons who were elected to office. The numbers probably
fluctuated from day to day but the official report contains no list of
delegates or numbers of those attending.

The full summaries of the proceedings that appeared in the morning
newspapers supplement the reports of the participants. From these reports it is evident that Walters did not mention all of the delegates—for
example, Mrs. J. J. Roberts, the aged widow of the first president of
Liberia, then living in London, whom Williams said was among the ladies with positions on the platform and who "distinguished themselves."
The Liberal *News* said the purpose of the conference was "to voice the
opinions of black men throughout the world, to unite and organize them
for the attainment of equality and freedom, and to influence legislation
in their favor."

Williams, to whom Walters credited "the idea of a convocation of
Negro representatives from all parts of the world," [9] said later with
obvious pride that they met "as never before did colored people meet in
their lives and assailed London with a conference." [10]

The conference was not universally welcomed. An arrogant contributor to the evening *Pall Mall Gazette* thought it a waste of time. He argued,
speciously, that blacks had failed to utilize opportunities given them
since emancipation in the Americas and concluded that they were "in-
capable of raising [themselves] no matter what the sentimentalists may
say to the contrary." [11]

Before the meeting began agreement was reached that Bishop Walters
should preside. As a forty-two-year-old prelate, a leader in the African
Methodist Episcopal Zion church in the United States, and president of
the National Afro-American Council, he was the most distinguished

participant. Although his name is conspicuously absent from Booker T. Washington's *New Negro for a New Century* (1900), the *Colored American* (Washington, D.C.) wrote of him "in the same breath" as it did of the great Mr. Washington. The paper praised his breadth of vision and liberal heart and acclaimed him "one of the most notable figures of this generation."[12] After the conference, the *Colored American,* reporting his presidency of the Pan-African Association and honorary membership of the New Reform Club, called Bishop Walters "one of the ablest, best known and most popular Negro divines in this country."[13] Bishop Walters was already well known in church circles in England, too, having participated in religious conferences and preached in Methodist churches there in 1889, 1890, and 1891.

Flanking him on the platform were the representatives of two independent African states—Frederick Johnson, former attorney-general of Liberia, and Sylvain, noticed by all the newspapers as the Emperor Menelik's aide-de-camp and described by one as "a picturesque figure of the conference."[14] Du Bois, writing twenty years later, recalled Sylvain as "the stiff, young officer who came with credentials from Menelik of Abyssinia."[15] Professor John Love of Washington, D.C., was elected secretary of the conference, and two committees were named.[16] One was to consider and report on the formation of a permanent Pan-African Association and the other, to which Du Bois was elected chairman, was to draw up an address to the nations of the world.[17]

The secretary read letters from invitees who could not attend. One came from the bishop of Hereford, Rt. Rev. John Perceval, who, only two weeks earlier, had presided over a conference convened by the Aborigines Protection Society, "The Native Question in South Africa." Bishop Perceval was a liberal-minded prelate as his address at the A. P. S. meeting showed.[18]

The conference opened in the absence of the bishop of London, Walters announcing that Dr. Creighton, who would deliver the address of welcome, would not arrive until later. Walter's opening address, described as "a model of forensic deliverance," dealt thoughfully with "The Trials and Tribulations of the Colored Race in America" and set the tone of the conference. For the first time in history, he said, blacks had gathered from all parts of the globe to discuss how to improve the condition of the race, to assert the rights of blacks and to organize them so that they might take an equal place among nations. In the United States it had been their misfortune to live among a people whose laws, traditions, and prejudices had always been against blacks. It had taken the black two hundred years to gain personal emancipation and one hundred years to attain standing as a soldier. It would hardly be expected, therefore, that he would get his complete social and political rights in thirty-five years. The black people in the United States had been able neverthless to eliminate 45 percent of their illiteracy and they now owned $735 million in real estate and personal property. And they were now engaged in a long and severe struggle for full social and political rights.

The first paper, read by C. W. French of St. Kitts, claimed equality for blacks. Entitled "Conditions Favoring a High Standard of African Humanity," it exposed the inequities accorded blacks living under British rule and demanded equality for black people.

The cultural aspects were dealt with in a "clever and thoughtful" paper presented by Anna H. Jones of Kansas. In "The Preservation of Race Individuality," she argued that it was important to preserve the identity of the black race and develop its artistic talents.[19]

The guest speaker arrived promptly at noon and was cordially received by the assembly, which rose to welcome him. The two bishops were not strangers to one another; Bishop Walters had recently opened one of the meetings of the International Christian Endeavor Convention at which Bishop Creighton was one of the guest speakers. Dr. Creighton told the gathering of blacks that providence had placed weighty responsibilities on the British people for the welfare of other races, and they must move forward to confer on those races as soon as possible the benefits of self-government that they themselves enjoyed.

Sylvain's paper, given at the evening meeting, "The Necessary Concord to be Established between Native Races and European Colonists," was an outspoken anticolonialist attack. His country, Haiti, had fought its way to freedom to the dismay of the slave-owning world and had resisted North American encroachment, while Abyssinia, whose emperor he represented, had repulsed a European power. In his view, the capital of the British empire had been rightly chosen as their meeting place. He blamed the British people particularly for the antiliberal reaction that had characterized the colonial policy of the last fifteen years. The British government had tolerated the most frightful deeds of the chartered companies, he declared. But not too many years in the future, the rights of the indigenous peoples would have to be recognized by

every colonial power. These people, he said, must no longer be considered as serfs, taxable and workable at their masters' whim, but as
indispensable elements in the prosperity of the colonies and, therefore,
with equitable participation in the material and mental profits of
colonization. No one, Sylvain asserted, could stop the Africans in their
social and political development. The question now was whether Europe
would accept this improvement, which was essentially against her interests. The Pan-African Association, which must emerge from the conference, would assist in the realization of peaceful social and political
advancement for Africa. Then Mrs. Anna J. Cooper, of Washington,
D.C., read a paper on "The Negro Problem in America," which the
Leader described as "pathetic" in an America that called itself Christian.

The morning of the second day was devoted to reading and discussing
two papers. First, Frederick Johnson led a discussion, "The Progress of
Our People in the Light of Current History," in which he extolled
Africans for their bravery, their industry, and their capacity for self-
government. The growth of the Liberian republic had been established in
the face of the antagonism of unscrupulous white traders who hated all
restraint of the law, especially from black people. John E. Quinlan of
St. Lucia complained that the money contributed by the English people
for the relief of sufferers in the West Indies hurricane of 1898 had been
unequally distributed among whites and blacks. He charged that the aim
of the British capitalists was to enslave the black people in South Africa
and called on the English people to complete the great act of justice
that they had commenced with the abolition of slavery.

William Meyer, the next speaker, was a Trinidadian medical student
at Edinburgh University and one of the two delegates of the Afro-West
Indian Literary Society there. This "quiet, intellectual young African"
rebutted the pronouncements of European "race philosophers" that
the Negro was not a man but an entity just a stage above an ape and
that he was depraved and worthless. Richard Phipps, another Trinidadian,
spoke about nonwhites in his country. He claimed that the worst positions in the civil service were set aside for them, and if they were appointed it was on the understanding that their actions would be controlled.

The second topic was "Africa, the Sphinx of History in the Light of
Unsolved Problems," and the leading speaker was D. E. Tobias. He may
have been the black American (mentioned by Du Bois) who "whispered

how an army of the Soudan might some day cross the Alps." [20] Speaking on the Boer war, he said people must ensure that at the end of it the vile principles which made war possible were removed. Du Bois, the next speaker, emphasized "the ignoble fact," as the *Leader* termed it, that nowhere were blacks able to maximize their potential. It was patent, he said, that this was not simply an injustice and a hindrance to blacks; it hindered human evolution.

The Rev. Henry Smith, whose contribution was reported only in the *Leader,* advanced the theory that Adam had been a black man and that Africans had started civilization after the flood. It was ancient Ethiopia, he maintained, that gave the great stimulus to Egyptian civilization, which in due course affected the life of Greece. Smith cited Homer, Herodotus, Pliny, Josephus, and others in support of his thesis and, according to the reporter, he did not "sternly and critically distinguish" between history and mythology, insisting that mythology had a meaning. He foresaw that the future history of the African would be grand and glorious and they would be unwise if they permitted any differences in the various shades of color of black people to interfere with their progress. Whether black or quadroon or octoroon, they should all work together. After Chaplain B. W. Arnett and Professor T. J. Calloway had spoken, the chairman announced that the delegates had been invited to tea by the bishop of London. It proved to be a welcome interlude.

Bishop Walters, a man with a streak of vanity as his autobiography shows, was most impressed with the bishop of London's "high tea" at his "stately mansion" at Fulham, the home of the bishops of London since the fifteenth century. He alone gave a description of the occasion, which he thought should be "long remembered." He remarked on the delegates' being greeted by "His Lordship and one or two other Bishops with their wives and daughters," their being served a "magnificent repast," and being conducted through the extensive palace grounds. He made special mention of "Professor Du Bois, M. Benito Sylvain, Messrs. Downing and Calloway, Miss Jones and others," who "moved about the palace and grounds with such a surprising ease and elegance" that "one would have thought they were 'to the manor [*sic*] born.' " [21]

In the evening the delegates went back to their papers and discussions, which were "interspersed with musical selections." It is likely that Samuel Coleridge Taylor, the black English pianist and composer who at twenty-five was already famous, and J. F. Loudin, director of the Fisk Jubilee Singers, and Mrs. Loudin, who were delegates, contributed to the musical program. But it was Sylvain whom a newspaper reporter selected for mention as contributing "the chief musical feature"—a tribute to the Haitian's versatility.

Opening the meeting on the third and final day, Bishop Walters spoke briefly in recognition of the services whites in England and the United States rendered to the cause of black people. Then George J. Christian (Dominica) led a discussion on the theme, "Organized Plunder and Human Progress Have Made of Our Race Their Battlefield." In a wide-ranging survey of conditions in Africa, Christian declared that in the past Africans had been kidnapped from their native country; now they were being jostled off their land. In South Africa, where the Boer farmer looked on Africans as beasts of burden inferior to other humans, they were not allowed to travel without a pass, no matter what their wealth, character, or intelligence might be. For them the franchise was out of the question. In Rhodesia they were compelled to work for inadequate wages; the chiefs were forced to find gangs of black men for the mines, where they had to work for months at the absolute mercy of their white employers. This, he said, was a revival of slavery and degrading to black people. Christian was pessimistic about the coming settlement between the British and Afrikaners in South Africa and forecast that the Africans would receive scant consideration from the white colonizers. To defeat this he called for "guaranteed protection by laws which no colonial legislature could alter and no prejudiced judge pervert" and, in addition, the creation of reserves for Africans with some measure of home rule by the chiefs over the tribes.

Henry F. Downing (United States) declared that blacks had no intention of complying with the wishes of those who desired them to remain slaves forever. Charles P. Lee (United States) thought the black man's problem could be solved by the acquisition of property and of solid and substantial knowledge in order to be able to compete with the white man in every department of life. He was followed by Felix Moschelles, who may have come from Cape Colony, [22] and finally by Williams who declared that it was time that blacks issue a protest against the treatment of colored people in South Africa.

In closing the discussion, Bishop Walters said the object was to secure moral, political, and civil rights for blacks. They had the force of numbers on their side; the conference was just the beginning of the work, and it meant that blacks throughout the world would organize for their own betterment.

It had been contemplated before the meeting that a permanent Pan-African Association should be formed. The first committee report read and adopted at the afternoon session recommended the formation of such an organization with headquarters in London and branches overseas. The association would convene in general meeting every second year in some large city in Europe or America or an independent black state. The next meeting would be held in the United States in 1902 and that for 1904 in Haiti to add to the solemnity of the centenary celebration of Haitian freedom.[23] The African Association was declared merged into the new Pan-African Association, and it was agreed that other organizations already in existence whose aims were similar to those of the Pan-African Association would be readily affiliated on formal application to the executive.

The aims and objects of the Pan-African Association were:

1. To secure to Africans throughout the world true civil and political rights.
2. To ameliorate the condition of our brothers on the continent of Africa, America and other parts of the world.
3. To promote efforts to secure effective legislation and encourage our people in educational, industrial and commercial enterprise.
4. To foster the production of writing and statistics relating to our people everywhere.
5. To raise funds for forwarding these purposes. [24]

The conference then proceeded to elect officers who were to hold office for two years. The official list follows:

The Right Rev. Alexander Walters, M.A., D.D., *President*
The Rev. Henry B. Brown, *Vice-President*
Dr. R. J. Colenso, M.A., *General Treasurer*
M. Benito Sylvain, *General Delegate for Africa*
H. Sylvester Williams, Esq., *General Secretary*

EXECUTIVE COMMITTEE
Hon. Henry F. Downing, S. Coleridge Taylor, Esq., A.R.C.M.,
F. J. Loudin, Esq., J. R. Archer, Esq., Mrs. Jane Cobden Unwin,
Mrs. Anna J. Cooper, M.A.[25]

The conference also nominated and elected officers of branches overseas as follows:

> U.S.A.—Vice-President: Dr. W. E. B. Du Bois; Secretary: T. J.
> Calloway.
> Haiti—Vice-President: M. A. Firmin; Secretary: Right Rev. Dr. Holly.
> Abyssinia—Vice-President: M. Benito Sylvain; Secretary: Dr.
> R. A. K. Savage, M.R.C.P.
> Liberia—Vice-President: Hon. F. E. R. Johnson; Secretary:
> S. F. Dennis, Esq.
> South Africa:
>   Natal—Vice-President: Edwin Kinloch, Esq.
> West Africa:
>   Sierra Leone—Vice-President: J. A. Williams, Esq., J.P.;
>   Secretary: M. Lewis, Esq.
>   Lagos—Vice-President: J. Otonba Payne, Esq.; Secretary:
>   N. W. Holm, Esq.
> British West Indies:
>   Jamaica—Vice-President: Hon. H. R. Cargill.[26]

According to the report of the conference, it was hoped that
branches would be established in Cape Town, Rhodesia, Gold Coast, Trinidad, Canada, Orange River Colony, and Transvaal, but there is no evidence that any were established except in Jamaica and Trinidad. A note in
the report invited active or honorary members who desired to attend
the conference to be held in the United States in 1902 to write early
to the general secretary.

The conference decided, among other things, to invite the heads
of three black sovereign states to accept honorary membership in the
association; they were the Emperor Menelik of Abyssinia, President
Simon Sam of Haiti, and President Joseph Coleman of Liberia. Sylvain,
who had been in touch with both the emperor and the president of
Haiti and described himself as delegate of Haiti and Ethiopia, gave a

different version from that contained in the conference report. He described the three heads of state as "Grand Protectors," suggesting a position more exalted than honorary membership and more akin to patronage, and so more befitting heads of state. [27]

The conference evidently gave thought to the idea of cooperation between the three black states (Abyssinia, Haiti, and Liberia), for Sylvain stated that a memorial was to be addressed to these heads of state drawing their attention to the urgent necessity of consolidating their interests and combining their efforts in the diplomatic field. This was in reaction to what Sylvain described as the politics of extermination and degradation that prevailed in Europe with respect to black people and their descendants. [28] Perhaps this was a secret decision of the conference committee or perhaps it was thought unnecessary to report more than the decisions of the conference for there is no such reference in the report. However, the distances separating the three states and the absence of opportunities for concerted action would have made a decision of the kind of doubtful value.

Next, the conference unanimously adopted an "Address to the Nations of the World" to be sent to the sovereigns in whose states subjects of African descent lived. In this address—signed by Walters, Brown, Williams, and Du Bois, as chairman of the "Committee on Address"—is to be found the prophetic phrase, "The problem of the Twentieth Century is the problem of the color line," which, in refined form, appeared later in Du Bois's *The Souls of Black Folk* (1903) as, "The problem of the Twentieth Century is the problem of the color line, the relation of the darker to the lighter races of men in Asia and Africa, in America and the islands of the sea." [29]

The address was a plea to the "great Powers of the civilized world," expressing trust in "the wide spirit of humanity and the deep sense of justice of our age," and calling for an end to color and race prejudice. It is not clear whether it was sent to specific nations, but its terms were directed generally to all nations and specifically to Great Britain, which had the largest number of black people under its rule, the United States, Germany, France, and Belgium. But though it included this appeal to the British nation, the delegates also sent a separate memorial to Queen Victoria calling for an end to the discrimination against nonwhites in South Africa.

The "Address to the Nations" called on Great Britain to give "as soon as practicable the rights of responsible government to the black colonies of Africa and the West Indies." This was a plea for equality of treatment with the white colonies of Australia, Canada, and New Zealand and the white-dominated colonies of Cape Colony and Natal, made perhaps with little appreciation that the discrimination was based solely on the grounds of race and color; Chamberlain, the colonial secretary, regarded blacks of the West Indies as "totally unfit for representative institutions." [30]

The phrase "responsible government" is a term of British constitutional law, familiar to Williams and to the other law students and barristers at the conference. It was in general application at the time to the fully self-governing British colonies. By having a cabinet or executive council responsible to the legislature, on whose confidence it relied for its existence, these colonies were distinguishable from those on a lower level having representative institutions or the others, lower still, that had no element of representation. It should be noted that the address did not speak of "the responsibility of self-government," as Elliott M. Rudwick claims, a phrase that he has taken from the speech of the bishop of London and that does not mean "responsible government." [31] Nor did the phrase in the address mean independence, as R. W. Logan seems to think in claiming that Du Bois "transformed Williams's aims to mean self-government or independence." [32] The "responsible government colonies," [33] as they were called then and much later, were not independent states; they were subordinate to the British Parliament, which could legislate for them in certain fields. Indeed "colony" and "independence" are mutually exclusive terms (a colony has no international status). In fact, examination of the principles declared by Du Bois's 1919 Pan-African Congress as those by which "the natives of Africa and the peoples of African descent" must be governed shows that they constituted a backward step rather than a transformation of aims. [34] And the same applies to subsequent congresses Du Bois called.

The "Address to the Nations" called on the United States to protect the American Negro from oppression and to grant him "the right of franchise" and "security of person and property." It called on the German empire and France to treat their black subjects with impartial justice, which, it said, was the first element of prosperity. It called for the "Congo Free State" of King Leopold to "become a great central Negro State of the world," but there is nothing to show that the delegates went any further in elaborating their ideas.

Sylvain related that the assistance of the Pan-African Association was sought, apparently in 1901, in the case of some Congolese who desired to return to their homeland after thirty years of slavery in Cuba. The association was contacted by Father Emanuel, who had gone to Belgium from Cuba in March 1901 to negotiate with the government of King Leopold II the repatriation of these Congolese Cubans (there were 1,000 to 1,500 involved). Four of them had visited the Congo with Father Emanuel in 1897 and were so impressed that they intended to return with their wives and children. But Father Emanuel's mission to Brussels was not successful, and he agreed, evidently after discussion with Sylvain, to postpone a decision until the Pan-African Conference in the United States in August or September 1902. In reporting this, Sylvain indignantly referred to the "imperfect nature" of Leopold's *rights* over the Congo, saying they were always contestable and would never be recognized. [35]

Finally, the "Address to the Nations" called on the imperialistic nations to respect the integrity and independence of "the free Negro States of Abyssinia, Liberia, Haiti, etc." [36]

The conference had planned to send a memorial to the British government on the ill-treatment of Africans and coloreds in South Africa but, with the permission of the prime minister, the marquess of Salisbury, [37] it was sent directly to Queen Victoria. It said that the Pan-African Conference "comprising men and women of African blood and descent" respectfully invited her "august and sympathetic attention to the fact that the situation of the native races in South Africa is causing us and our friends alarm." They listed the causes of their alarm:

1. The degrading and illegal compound system of native labor in vogue in Kimberley and Rhodesia.
2. The so-called indenture, i.e., legalized bondage of native men, women and children to white colonists.
3. The system of compulsory labor on public works.
4. The "pass" or docket system used for people of color.
5. Local bye-laws tending to segregate and degrade the natives—such as the curfew, the denial to the natives of the use of the foot

paths; and the use of separate public conveyances.
6. Difficulties in acquiring real property.
7. Difficulties in obtaining the franchise. [38]

In the prayer accompanying the address they asked that these conditions be remedied.

At the close of their historic meeting, the delegates adjourned to the terrace of the House of Commons for tea as guests of Dr. Gavin Clark, the Liberal MP. It was the last of a round of functions arranged by Williams in their honor, which had included a luncheon at the Liberal Club hosted by H. R. Fox-Bourne, honorary secretary of the Aborigines Protection Society and an honorary member of the African Association. The men delegates were admitted into the House of Commons itself, a privilege that was denied to women who, like the mass of black colonials, were voteless. The delegates reconvened later for a musical evening, and C. W. French and the chairman of the Pan-African Conference committee, Rev. H. Mason Joseph, delivered speeches, which wound up the conference program.

Williams was well satisfied with the attention the conference received. It was adequately reported in the leading London newspapers, though they offered no editorial comment, perhaps because it was a phenomenon whose significance was beyond the grasp of the policy makers or because it raised questions they were chary to discuss. Easily the most extensive notice of the conference in a British journal was in the *Review of Reviews*. The participants had called for the recognition of the human rights of all blacks and had spoken of achieving their aims by constitutional means. Leading publicist W. T. Stead, editor of the widely read and influential *Review of Reviews,* interpreted the conference as part of the worldwide revolt of colored people against white domination. Stead (whom Williams met a few years later and impressed sufficiently to merit a *Review of Reviews* interview) gave star billing in his August 1900 issue to the conference. He chose it as his "Topic of the Month" under the heading, "The Revolt Against the Paleface," and he devoted five pages to it. Stead reminded his readers that the Italians had been defeated by Menelik and noted that the Ethiopian emperor had been made an honorary member of the Pan-African Association. [39] Stead concluded that the white world was face to face with a determined effort on the part of the colored races to assert their right to live their own lives in their own way without "the perpetual bullying of the Palefaces."

The conference did not go unnoticed elsewhere. Sylvain noted that the rare mention in the French press made it look as if it had been a "bizarre show."[40] Walters sent home a report, which was published in the *Colored American* along with stories taken from the London papers of the conference proceedings.[41] Notice was taken of it by the newspapers in Trinidad and in Lagos, where the *Lagos Standard* appealed to blacks throughout the world to support the Pan-African Association, "an institution which in its great and noble aspirations is so very deserving of their help, sympathy and encouragement."[42]

And so Bishop Walters, Du Bois, and other overseas delegates departed, leaving behind those like Williams and Christian who had to complete their studies. In reporting to American readers, Bishop Walters said, "Special mention should be made of the work done by Prof. Du Bois in London,"[43] but the notion that Du Bois dominated the conference seems to be more fancy than fact; there is no evidence to support such a view.[44] It is strange that Du Bois did not write about the conference or Williams for forty years, nor did he even mention them in his autobiographical works. In *Dusk of Dawn* (1940) the only event of 1900 he recalled was his participation in the Paris exposition,[45] which he singled out later as "a significant occurrence" in his life.[46] In the *Autobiography of W. E. B. Du Bois* (1968), the conference is mentioned only once, and that in an appended calendar of Du Bois's public life.[47] This calendar erroneously called Du Bois "secretary First Pan-African Conference in England." The official report mentions no such post but, according to Walters, John L. Love was elected conference secretary.[48]

In his writings, Du Bois claims that he originated the Pan-African idea. In *Dusk of Dawn* he says he took a "new" path after World War I in "the development of the idea back of the Pan-African Congress"[49] he called in Paris. In the *Autobiography* he wrote of having "emerged" with a program of pan-Africanism as "organized protection of the Negro world led by American Negroes."[50]

Not until 1945 did Du Bois recall Williams's connection with pan-Africanism. In a column, "The Winds of Time," in the *Chicago Defender,* he referred to the coining of the word "Pan-Africa" in the last year of the nineteenth century when Williams "called a

Pan-African Conference in London." [51] He said the conference
was "small but interesting" and composed chiefly of West Indians
with a few American Negroes, that the late Bishop Walters was
elected "permanent chairman," and he (Du Bois) was "secretary
for America" but that "no further effort took place for a generation." In fact there were a few more Americans than West Indians
listed by Walters as delegates, though it was the West Indians and
Africans who had convened and organized the conference.

In the preparatory volume for the *Encyclopedia of the Negro,*
edited by Du Bois and Guy B. Johnson for the Phelps-Stokes Fund
in 1946, Du Bois failed to mention the 1900 Pan-African Conference; he referred only to his own Pan-African Congresses. He remembered Williams and the 1900 conference again in *The World
and Africa* (1947)—a reference that is reproduced, slightly edited,
in George Padmore's *History of the Pan-African Congress*—and there
he said, "The movement and the idea died for a generation." [52]
When Du Bois wrote his *Autobiography,* he did not even mention
Walters in connection with pan-Africanism though the two men continued to be associated otherwise (in the National Association for
the Advancement of Colored People Walters was one of the two
vice-presidents on the first board). [53]

It would seem that Du Bois was not satisfied with his performance
at the 1900 conference and did not think much of the conference
itself. Though he was chairman of the drafting committee he never
claimed credit for the "Address to the Nations" to which much attention has been directed. His attitude suggests that his participation
was incidental and perfunctory. His statement that "no further effort
took place for a generation" is at once an exaggeration—for he was
thinking only in terms of another conference—and a confession of
failure in his organizational task in the United States. At a later date
he confessed to "inexperience with organizations"[54] even during the
existence of the Niagara movement, and there is no evidence that he did
anything as secretary or as vice-president for America of the Pan-African
Association. However, a reference has been found to a Pan-African
League Department of the Niagara Movement, [55] further evidence that
the Pan-African idea had not died after 1900.

The prevailing climate in the United States immediately after the
conference may not have been propitious for pan-Africanism. The

Colored American in 1901 conceded that the Pan-African Association "ought to secure a foothold" in the United States but qualified this by adding that the Afro-American, who indeed was involved in a life and death struggle,[56] must take care of himself and not leave it to others.[57]

There is no basis for the proposition that pan-Africanism entailed the abandonment by blacks in the United States of their own fight for equal rights, leaving it to be fought by "others." Walters did not see it in this light. He believed that the Pan-African Association and the National Afro-American Council, efficiently officered and wisely managed, could do a great deal to better the condition of blacks throughout the world.[58] Nor would Williams have seen it any differently for he invariably spoke of blacks anywhere as "our people," "our brothers," or "oppressed brethren in Africa," not as "others." To borrow from Frederick Douglass—who was speaking of liberty—Williams, in matters of race, saw "no geographical lines" and "no national limitations."[59]

Du Bois lamented that American Negroes were "not interested," when, twenty years after the London conference, he "emerged" with a program for pan-Africanism as "organized protection of the Negro world, led by American Negroes."[60] Evidently the London conference had left him unimpressed and in this he was unlike Stead, who feared the possible consequences, or Walters, who saw in the "great awakening on the part of Negroes" abundant proof that the inauguration of a "great international as well as national organization" was timely,[61] or Williams, who soon set about carrying out the conference decisions with great enthusiasm.

When the conference ended, the task of directing the new Pan-African Association fell largely on the members of the executive committee resident in London. To Williams fell the duty of arranging for the submission of the memorial to Queen Victoria and of despatching the "Address to the Nations," the memorials to Emperor Menelik and the presidents of Liberia and Haiti, the resolutions passed, and the letters of thanks for assistance given. But it was not until August 30 that Williams wrote the British and Foreign Anti-Slavery Society, forwarding a copy of the resolution expressing appreciation of the society's work.[62] In the interval between the conference and despatch of the letter, he had traveled to Paris to attend the Anti-

Slavery Congress on August 6, 7, and 8, convened by the French
Anti-Slavery Society in connection with the Paris exposition. [63]

The Congress met in the Palais de Congrès on the exposition site under the presidency of the venerable and distinguished Senator Henri
Wallon, the author of *History of Slavery in Ancient Times*. [64] Williams,
through Sylvain, probably met Anténor Firmin, then Haitian minister to
France, who had been elected vice-president for Haiti of the Pan-African
Association. Williams probably spoke at the congress, which some nonwhites attended. Sylvain spoke, apparently injecting much feeling into
his contribution to the discussions, unlike the white participants who
read papers on the contemporary slave trade in the African colonies and
protectorates of the European powers and in the Middle East. An
English report observed that Sylvain's speech was delivered "with some
warmth" as he dwelt on the indifference and contempt with which he
believed the majority of Europeans regarded black people—"a statement
which produced exclamations of dissent" from the audience. [65] Sylvain's intervention must have been dramatic indeed for when, four years
later, after he had obtained his doctorate in law from the University of
Paris, he addressed the Geographical Society of Toulouse, the president
referred to his brilliant addresses at the Brussels and Paris antislavery
congresses. [66]

According to the conference report which Williams prepared between
completing his studies for the bar final examination and the Paris visit,
the association had already established "permanent headquarters" with
"a Bureau from which it hopes to disseminate facts and statistics relating to the circumstances and conditions of members of the African
race wherever found." [67] The report emphasized that the association
officers wished the association to be self-supporting and not dependent
on white people for financial support. They planned that it should be
"independent and unhampered" in every way and called on "members
of the race" to support it with their means and influence. [68]

Along with the memorial to Queen Victoria and the "Address to the
Nations," the report contains the text of the conference relolutions. One
thanks the Anti-Slavery Society for its "great and noble work . . . for the
abolition of slavery in the West Indies, Africa, the United States and
Brazil." Others thanked the Native Races and Liquor Traffic United
Committee for its "noble efforts" for the amelioration of the condition
of native races and for the suppression of the "iniquitous" traffic in

liquor among them; the Aborigines Protection Society for the protection afforded the aboriginal inhabitants of the British empire and other countries; and the Society of Friends for its "indefatigable labors" in the cause of emancipation in the West Indies, the United States, Brazil, and other places. The report noted the conference's "marked appreciation of the unselfish sacrifice" even then being exercised by the Society of Friends in Pemba and Zanzibar for those still "enslaved under the British flag."

The report also expressed the conference's gratitude to the "many friends and societies" who had encouraged Williams, as honorary secretary of the African Association, to bring about "this eventful epoch." It trusted that the friends would still continue to show goodwill so that they could perfect their plans for a bureau enabling them to "further influence public opinion" and make "authentic" representations to the authorities in matters affecting the welfare of the race all over the globe.[69]

Financially the conference was not a success. Williams solicited and received contributions from persons whom he thought would be sympathetic. Among the contributors were English people of varying backgrounds in addition to the participants in the conference or members of the African Association. Some of the sympathizers can be identified. Among them were the Rev. F. B. Meyer, head of the National Free Church Council; Frederick Courtenay Selous, better known as a big game hunter, a former officer of the Buluwayo Field Force, and author of several books on southern Africa, including *Sunshine and Storm in Rhodesia*, a narrative of the Matabele war; Arthur E. Pease, a Liberal MP and sportsman who visited Emperor Menelik in 1901 as he reported in his book, *Travel and Sport in Africa* (1902); Sir George Williams, founder of the Young Men's Christian Association and lessee of Exeter Hall; Catherine Impey, the social reformer, editor of *Anti-Caste*, and correspondent of John E. Bruce (Bruce Grit), and her sister; Miss Adams, mentioned only by Sylvain as being present at the conference and said to have come from Ireland; and Miss Balgarnie, possibly the same person mentioned as one of the speakers at the annual meeting of the Liberation Society in 1897. [70] Familiar names among the contributors included those of Travers Buxton, secretary of the Anti-Slavery Society, and H. R. Fox-Bourne, secretary of the Aborigines Protection Society. There were several clergymen and others with religious connections among the other contributors.

An interesting and perhaps significant contributor was Dadabhai Naoroji who gave ten shillings. Naoroji, a Parsi prominent in the work of national reconstruction in India, has been described as "not only India's first great statesman but also as the first Indian economist to lay the foundation of an Indian school of economic thought."[71] He had been living and working in England for many years and was the first Indian elected to the British Parliament.[72] Naoroji, who was then president of the London Indian Society, had presided over the Indian National Congress at Lahore in 1893 and was to preside, in his declining years, over the Congress at Calcutta in 1906. Evidently Naoroji, of whom it was said that "the Congress in its early years owed more to [his] faithful work . . . in London than any other single person,"[73] saw some affinity between his work for the Indian people and what Williams was trying to do for Africans at home and abroad. His work in and out of Parliament inspired Williams to seek to do the same for his own people, fellow Britishers in Africa and the West Indies.[74]

The conference accounts, made up to August 31, showed a deficit of about twenty-two pounds with expenses totaling just over one hundred pounds. The main items of expenditure were printing, a special reporter, postage during the period 1898 to 1900, and stationery. It is not known to whom the unpaid balance was due or if it was ever settled, but the lack of funds was to give rise to a split in the association.

It was not until September that Williams submitted the memorial to Queen Victoria. The engrossing may have taken time though there may have been other reasons for the delay. At the time the queen was in residence at Balmoral in Scotland, and Williams surmised that it was despatched to her there. He later claimed that at a meeting of the Privy Council she instructed Colonial Secretary Chamberlain to reply to the memorial, but the rest of the year went by without any reply.[75]

Examination time for Williams came in mid-October. The bar examinations were held from October 16 to 18, and Williams at last took the final papers. His name appeared in the pass list published November 2.

Had Williams been diligent in the ritual of keeping term he might have been called to the bar on November 19. To keep a term, a student who was also attached to a university was required to dine three times in hall in each of the year's four dining terms; for nonuniversity students the requirement was six times a term. Possibly because of frequent absences from London, Williams was two terms short. He petitioned the masters of the bench asking for a dispensation of these terms, but the benchers, probably well aware that he had been dividing his time between the cause of his people and his studies, refused.[76] It was to be a long time before he would be called to the bar.

It was out of concern about the "acute ill-treatment of the natives of South Africa" that the Pan-African Conference had decided to send a memorial to the queen. The London members of the executive committee were disturbed, therefore, that no reply had come. However, they went about their other business. Taking cognizance of the approach of the new century, the committee decided to mark it by issuing a "New Century Letter." In it they called attention to the aims and objects of the association and to the successful efforts of Europeans and Americans, which had "placed us upon the platform of freedom." The committee urged its members to recognize these advances and "occupy . . . positions as real factors and producers in the progress of civilization." They noticed "with marked satisfaction" the attainments and aspirations of blacks in the British colonies, the United States, Haiti, Liberia, Brazil, Abyssinia, Cuba, and the Philippines, and they were "sanguine of the future." On the other hand there had been instances of retrogression in British territory, in the United States, Congo Free State, German territory in Africa, Pemba, Zanzibar, and Portuguese territory, which called for determined and organized efforts to right the situation "by constitutional means."

The dawn of the twentieth century, the letter continued, would demand alertness in every sphere, and every member was expected to be active. The executive suggested that every able black should associate in city, town, and village to form association branches. Finally, they called for "authentic and bonafide" reports on matters affecting the welfare of "our people" under the various governments for dissemination and so to instruct public opinion.[77]

A few months later Williams claimed that the letter had been sent to "our people" wherever an organized Pan-African Association branch had been established and asserted, perhaps exaggeratingly, "We had branches throughout the length and breadth of the British Empire."[78] It was then that he related what happened about the memorial to the Queen. At a meeting on January 11 of the executive committee, Mrs. Cobden Unwin raised the question of the memorial, saying she felt something was amiss; that the sovereign would not be so discourteous as not to reply to a memorial. So, acting on instructions, Williams wrote to the queen the same evening, enquiring whether she had received the memorial. On January 17 Williams received a letter from Chamberlain's secretary saying Mr. Secretary Chamberlain had received "the Queen's commands to inform you that the memorial of the Pan-African Association regarding the situation of the native races in South Africa has been laid before her Majesty and that she was graciously pleased to command him to return an answer to it on behalf of her Government." Chamberlain desired him to assure the members of the Pan-African Conference that "in settling the lines on which the administration of the conquered territories is to be conducted, Her Majesty's Government will not overlook the interests of the native races." The letter added that a copy of the memorial had been sent to the high commissioner in South Africa. [79]

Gratified at the reply and at the promise that "the interests of the native races" would not be overlooked, Williams immediately issued the text to the newspapers. It appeared in *The Times* the following day under the headline, "The South African Native Question," with an introductory paragraph referring to the conference as having been "attended by men and women of African blood and descent" and to the general secretary as "The Rev. Henry Sylvester Williams."[80] However, the memorial had dealt with conditions among the natives in South Africa generally, but Chamberlain's reply referred only to the so-called settlement in the "conquered territories," namely, Transvaal and Orange River. It was not a direct reply to the memorial. Was it a genuine error or a politician's trick? It said not one word of the compound system, compulsory labor, the pass system, the segregation of natives, the denial of property rights, or denial of the franchise, the grievances they wished to be redressed.

Yet Williams saw in the queen's commands to Chamberlain to reply to the memorial her interest in colored people. Shortly after the reply reached Williams, Queen Victoria died. Her passing marked the end of an era in which her empire had been built and expanded by robbery and deceit, by forced labor and murder, by wresting from less advanced people their land and their wealth.

Williams, Anglophile that he was, felt that black people had reason for pride and for revering the memory of Victoria "because her first act on ascending the throne was the absolute emancipation of their people and her very last act was in connection with them,"[81] He was, however, to see the day when it would be plain that the promise that her majesty's government would not overlook the interests of the native races in South Africa was not worth the paper it was written on.

NOTES

1. A. P. Thornton, *The Imperial Idea and Its Enemies* (New York: St. Martin's Press, 1959), p. 108.

2. William L. Langer, *The Diplomacy of Imperialism, 1890-1902* (New York: Alfred Knopf, 1951), pp. 88-96.

3. Benito Sylvain, *Du Sort des Indigènes dans les Colonies d'Exploitation* (Paris: Boyer, 1901).

4. Alexander Walters, *My Life and Work* (New York: Fleming H. Revel Company, 1917), p. 260.

5. *Colored American,* August 25, 1900.

6. *Mirror,* June 1, 1901.

7. W. E. B. Du Bois, *Darkwater* (New York: Schocken Press, 1969), p. 193.

8. *Report of the Pan-African Conference at Westminster Town Hall, 1900* (London: The Pan-African Association, 1900), p. 16.

9. Walters, *My Life and Work,* p. 253.

10. *Mirror,* June 1, 1901.

11. *Pall Mall Gazette,* July 24, 1900.

12. *Colored American,* March 10, 1901.

13. Ibid., September 8, 1900.

14. *Daily Leader,* quoted in *Colored American,* August 11, 1900.

15. Du Bois, *Darkwater,* p. 193.

16. Walters, *My Life and Work,* p. 255.

17. *Report of the Pan-African Conference, 1900,* p. 12.

18. *The Times,* July 4, 1900.

19. *Colored American,* August 11, 1900.

20. Du Bois, *Darkwater,* p. 193.

21. "And to the manner born." Shakespeare, *Hamlet,* act 1, sc. 4, line 15.

22. Du Bois mentions Cape Colony as being represented at the conference; see Du Bois, *Darkwater,* p. 193.

23. Sylvain, *Du Sort des Indigènes,* p. 511.

24. *Colored American,* February 1, 1901.

25. *Report of the Pan-African Conference, 1900,* p. 18.

26. Ibid. pp. 13-14.

27. Sylvain, *Du Sort des Indigènes,* p. 511.

28. Ibid.

29. *Report of the Pan-African Conference, 1900*, p. 11.

30. Chamberlain to Dilke, April 16, 1896, quoted in H. A. Will, *Constitutional Change in the British West Indies* (Oxford: Clarendon Press, 1970), p. 232.

31. Elliott M. Rudwick, *W. E. B. Du Bois, A Study in Minority Race Leadership* (Philadelphia: University of Pennsylvania Press, 1960), pp. 208-209.

32. R. W. Logan, "The Historical Aspects of Pan-Africanism, 1900-1945," in AMSAC, *Pan-Africanism Reconsidered* (Berkeley: University of California Press, 1962), p. 38.

33. A. B. Keith, *Responsible Government in the Dominions* (Oxford: Clarendon Press, 1910), I:96. Winston Churchill said in 1905, "We must retain over South Africa as over our other self-governing colonies a general control." *Annual Register* (London: Longmans, 1906), pp. 24-25.

34. *Crisis* (April 1919): 274, statement signed by Blaise Diagne as president and Du Bois as secretary. See also Colin Legum, *Pan-Africanism, A Short Political Guide* (New York: Praeger, 1963), pp. 151-152.

35. Sylvain, *Du Sort des Indigènes*, pp. 515-519.

36. *Report of the Pan-African Conference, 1900*, p. 12. Du Bois, in *A.B.C. of Color* (Berlin: Seven Seas Publishers, 1964), p. 23, has "and the rest" while Sylvain has "et du Maroc" [and of Morocco], which was then independent and so remained until 1912 when it was partitioned by France and Spain with the connivance of Britain. E. D. Morel, *Black Man's Burden* (Manchester: National Labour Press, 1920), pp. 73ff.

37. *Report of the Pan-African Conference, 1900*, p. 8.

38. Ibid., p. 9.

39. *Review of Reviews* (August 1900): 131-137.

40. Sylvain, *Du Sort des Indigènes*, p. 504.

41. *Colored American*, October 17, 1900.

42. *Lagos Standard*, October 10, 1900, quoted by Imanuel Geiss, *Panafrikanismus, Zur Geschichte Der Dekolonisation* (Frankfurt am Main: Europaische Verlagsanstalt, 1965), p. 388.

43. *Colored American*, August 25, 1900.

44. A. Meier and E. Rudwick, *From Plantation to Ghetto* (New York: Hill and Wang, 1970), p. 201n.

45. W. E. B. Du Bois, *Dusk of Dawn* (New York: Schocken Press, 1969), p. 222.

46. W. E. B. Du Bois, *Autobiography of W. E. B. Du Bois* (New York: International Publishers, 1968), pp. 220-221.

47. Ibid., p. 438.

48. Walters, *My Life and Work*, p. 255.

49. Du Bois, *Dusk of Dawn*, p. 43.

50. Du Bois, *Autobiography*, p. 289.

51. *Chicago Defender*, September 22, 1945.

52. W. E. B. Du Bois, *The World and Africa* (New York: International Publishers, 1965), p. 8.

53. Charles F. Kellogg, *N.A.A.C.P.* (Baltimore: Johns Hopkins Press, 1967), 1:91.

54. Du Bois, *Autobiography*, p. 253.

55. See entry 1492 dated March 25, 1907, Calendar of Manuscripts, Schomburg Collection, New York Public Library.

56. *Crisis*, 1 (January 1911) shows 107 lynchings in each of the years 1900 and 1901. From 1901 to 1928 there was no Negro representative in Congress.

57. *Colored American*, August 17, 1901.

58. Walters, *My Life and Work*, p. 262.

59. Frederick Douglass, *Life and Times of Frederick Douglass* (New York: Macmillan, 1962), p. 496.

60. Du Bois, *Autobiography*, p. 289.

61. Walters, *My Life and Work*, p. 263.

62. Williams to Buxton, August 30, 1900, Anti-Slavery Papers, Rhodes House Library, Oxford.

63. *Mirror*, May 27, 1901.

64. *L'Étoile Africaine* (July 1906): 42n.

65. *Anti-Slavery Reporter* (August-October 1900).

66. *Bulletin de la Société de Géographie de Toulouse, Année 24e* (Toulouse: E. Privat, 1905).

67. Williams to Buxton, October 10, 1900, Anti-Slavery Papers.

68. *Report of the Pan-African Conference, 1900*, p. 6.

69. Ibid.

70. Ibid., pp. 12-13. It listed the following members as deserving of mention for their contributions to the success of the conference: "Messrs. A. R. Hamilton (Jamaica), J. W. D. Worrell (Barbados), Dr. Savage, Afro-West Indian Lit. Soc., Edin., Rev. Thos. L. Johnson (Africa) and the Hon. Henry F. Downing." For "excellent service" to the conference it mentioned "S. Coleridge Taylor, A.R.C.M. [Associate of the Royal College of Music]." Worrell is not otherwise mentioned in connection with the conference. The Rev. Mr. Johnson, according to the letterhead of the Pan-African conference committee, was its vice-chairman.

71. *New Age*, April 29, 1897. Ida Wells-Barnett refers to a Miss Florence Balgarnie in connection with Lady Henry Somerset and the

first Anti-Lynching Society in Great Britain, p. 84 in *On Lynching* (1892; reprint ed., New York: Arno Press, 1969).

72. C. F. Andrews and Girija Mukerji, *Rise and Growth of the Congress in India* (London: Allen and Unwin, 1938), p. 159.

73. *Essays, Speeches, Addresses and Writings of Dadabbai Naoroji* (Bombay: Caxton Printing Works, 1887), p. 3.

74. Andrews and Mukerji, *Rise and Growth,* p. 60.

75. *Review of Reviews* (March 1905): 250.

76. Mirror, June 1, 1901. A. P. Thornton, *The Imperial Idea and Its Enemies* (New York: St. Martin's Press, 1959), p. 125.

77. Mr. P. C. Beddingham, Librarian, Gray's Inn, to the author, July 2, 1970.

78. *Colored American,* February 1, 1901.

79. *Mirror,* June 1, 1901.

80. *Times,* January 18, 1901.

81. *Mirror,* June 1, 1901.

"Spreading the Word": 6
Organizing in Jamaica,
Trinidad, and the
United States

Williams had thrown himself into the cause of Africa and his race with missionary zeal. Having achieved a measure of success with the African Association and brought the Pan-African Association to birth, he was now ready to begin organizing. He had completed his bar examinations and formal call could wait, so he planned a tour of Jamaica, Trinidad, and the United States to establish branches of the Pan-African Association and arouse interest in the movement. The Jamaica part of the tour, however, would have a dual purpose; while setting up branches of the association he would look into some business.

The sugar industry of the West Indies was still suffering from the effects of depression and low prices, and Jamaica had been turning more and more to growing bananas for export since the West India Royal Commission's visit in 1897. In fact, some of the island's parishes that had long grown sugar now grew almost nothing else but bananas. [1] In London Williams had met the planter and merchant Henry Richard Cargill, who had been vice-president of the Pan-African Association for Jamaica. Yet Cargill is not mentioned in connection with Williams's activities in Jamaica on behalf of the Pan-African Association and his business association with the Jamaican was to prove abortive. Williams and Arthur Barnard, a West Indian barrister of Gray's Inn, resident in London, had talked with Cargill about a plan to import bananas from Jamaica into Britain, and Williams was now to arrange with Cargill for fortnightly shipments of 10,000 bunches. They planned to form a company in London to deal in the import and sale of bananas, and Barnard, whose family ran a ship-coaling and chandlery business in his home of St. Lucia, was to finance the project. He advanced Williams thirty pounds just before Williams sailed for Jamaica, and this formed the subject of a lawsuit six years later, which Williams lost. [2] Williams, who had regarded the money as part of his expense account rather than as a loan, was required to repay the sum.

The people of African descent comprised the largest group in the Jamaica population, and it was the more enlightened of these that Williams hoped to interest in the Pan-African Association. William Pringle Livingstone, the editor of the only daily newspaper, the *Daily Gleaner,* whom Williams met soon after his arrival in Kingston in March 1901, described their political condition in his book, *Black Jamaica,* published two years earlier. The majority, he claimed, had never paid any attention to politics. Livingstone, a Scotsman who had lived ten years on the island, claimed that they did not understand the machinery of popular government. Whatever may have been his merits as a perceptive observer, Livingstone could not claim that the crown colony system was ever intended to educate any colonial subject in the governing of his country.

The voters' roll, then totaling some 30,000, comprised occupants of houses paying taxes of ten shillings or more a year. While a number of these were blacks, few took the trouble to vote at elections, so the Negro was a minor factor in determining public issues. In like manner there were few black faces to be seen among the hundreds of brown faces at political gatherings and only one-third of the voters were interested in voting at elections. Most of the actual voters were brown and white and thus formed "the political majority," as Livingstone put it. However, according to H. A. Will, the number of registered voters had fallen from 42,266 in 1893-1894 to 16,236 in 1900-1901 because of the imposition of the literacy test and other factors, such as difficult economic conditions, which led to nonpayment of taxes and placement on the poor relief roll, both of which disqualified voters.[3] Moreover, after 1893, anyone who wanted to register had to apply to the collector of taxes; previously registration had been automatic.

No wonder that Livingstone wrote that blacks had had nothing to do with the destiny of the country so far as that destiny was controlled by exercise of the franchise. "No black man," he added, "has yet entered the Legislative Council." In 1899, when Livingstone was writing, only three black men had been candidates and all had been unsuccessful. Indeed, the ruling classes would not have been happy at their election; Will shows that the governor, Sir Arthur Hemming, and the officials were urgently advising against the easing of certain parochial qualifications because otherwise "Kingston Lawyers & newspaper editors of a low type" would be elected. [4]

Livingstone's book, which had great influence on the clerks in the Colonial Office in London, was not universally acclaimed in Jamaica.[5] Among Livingstone's caustic critics was Dr. Joseph Robert Love, editor of the *Jamaica Advocate,* at whom Hemming's degrading reference to newspaper editors was directed because the governor feared his election to the council. To him Livingstone was an enemy of blacks. Love, a native of the Bahamas, whom Williams also met and who was to be the leader of the local Pan-African Association, had originally been ordained an Episcopalian minister in Buffalo, New York, where he gained a reputation as a preacher. He had then taken up the study of medicine, graduating from the University of Buffalo in 1878. [6] After practicing briefly in the United States, he had gone to Haiti as an Episcopalian clergyman under the black American nationalist, Bishop James Theodore Holly, who had settled there, thus putting into practice what he had preached, for he expected blacks to go and live in a country where whites could not cow them.

The Rev. Dr. Love clashed with his bishop[7] and as a result abandoned the ministry and, after serving in the Haitian army as a doctor during the Salomon presidency, had come to Jamaica with the president in 1889 when he was overthrown. He had then settled in practice as a physician. Like Bishop Holly, who was listed in the report of the Pan-African Conference as secretary for Haiti and who had attended one of the preparatory meetings before the conference, Love was an admirer of the Haitian people. What further part Bishop Holly played in any activities relating to the Pan-African Association at the local level in Haiti is obscure. But Love, who had already founded movements for the uplift of the Jamaica masses and who wrote trenchantly in his newspaper in their interest, was to be of great help to Williams and to become for a time the foremost champion in Jamaica of the Pan-African cause.

Williams probably had been in communication with Love before he arrived in Jamaica. The *Jamaica Advocate* carried a letter from him, on behalf of the Pan-African Association, protesting against "existing British slavery in South Africa" and expressing "the fear among

the natives" that it would become worse at the end of the Boer War.[8]
Then, calling for just treatment for those who had helped the British
cause, Williams gave vent to what probably was a bit of the socialist
feeling of the day (for the socialist Keir Hardie was his friend), saying,
"The capitalist hoards his ill-gotten gain, but the people must contribute
to the weal of the community."

Williams may have brought letters of introduction from A. R.
Hamilton, the sole Jamaican delegate at the conference, and from some
of his church and temperance colleagues. When he called on Livingstone,
probably in quest of publicity, he heard with consternation that the
black people in Jamaica had no grievances at all. He determined to find
out whether this was true. Wherever he went during his six weeks' stay,
traveling over the country, holding public meetings, and forming
branches of the association, he asked questions.

Dr. Love attended Williams's first meeting, held in St. George's
Schoolroom, Kingston, on March 28 at which he expressed his sympathy with the movement, but he did not address the meeting. In
fact, two days earlier the executive committee of the People's Convention,[9] one of his Negro uplift organizations, had agreed, after
hearing Williams, to affiliate with the Pan-African Association.

A "large audience" attended the meeting, according to the *Advocate*, and there were prominent people with Williams on the platform,
including Canon H. H. Kilburn, the rector of St. George's, who had
lent the schoolroom. Some of them spoke, including the Hon. Alexander
Dixon, the first black man to sit in the Legislative Council (he had been
elected with Love's backing).[10] Others were the Rev. A. James, Henry
Ford, Dr. J. J. Edwards of Spanish Town, and the Rev. T. Gordon
Somers, also of Spanish Town and secretary of the People's Convention.

The recently arrived acting colonial secretary, Sydney Olivier, presided. Williams had brought him letters of introduction from two of his
friends—Keir Hardie (for Olivier had been one of the original Fabian
socialist pamphleteers with George Bernard Shaw and Sidney Webb) and
Harold Cox, his brother-in-law, whom Williams knew as secretary of
the Cobden Society.

Olivier, already popular with Jamaicans because of his ready tongue
and liberal utterances, so monopolized the meeting that the *Gleaner*
devoted one column and a half to his introductory remarks and only a

single paragraph to Williams who, according to the *Jamaica Times,* had
"put his cause forcibly." In fact, Williams would have found it very
trying indeed to follow a chairman who was not only the center of
attention but who also questioned the feasibility of his objectives;
however sympathetic Olivier's attitude showed him to be to the
plight of the Jamaican masses, whom he thought a "childish people," he
was part of the ruling class and could not be expected to see things in
the same light as the secretary of the Pan-African Association.[11] His
friends would not have sent Williams to him, he said, unless he were
worthy of consideration, but he could not clearly see what could be the
reason for Williams's visit to the West Indies. He said that he was prone to
regard with some distrust any racial association, whether it was called
pan-African or Semitic or Celtic. Olivier was objecting in effect to a
black West Indian involving himself in the enlightenment of his own
people.

Williams made no attempt to counter Olivier's thesis or to enter into
an argument with his loquacious chairman. He concentrated instead on
documenting oppression and denial of rights in Africa, especially in
South Africa. Then he argued that if the Africans in Jamaica were so
well off and happy as not to need the Pan-African Association for themselves, they should respond to the needs of Africans elsewhere and
support an organization founded to meet those needs. On his return to
London, Williams, commenting on Olivier's address, wrote that associations had made Britain great, the people uniting to foster their public
and private interest. In like manner, he said, "my people" should organize wherever found.[12]

In its report of the meeting, Dr. Love's paper referred to Williams
as "a forceful, easy speaker" and mentioned his pet ambition as an aim
of the movement, namely, "to have a member of Parliament of African
blood in the House of Commons." Dr. Love spoke at Williams's next
meeting, held in Kingston on April 9 under the chairmanship of Daniel
Alleyne, described as the president of the Jamaica branch of the Pan-African Association. The other speakers included C. L. Campbell, editor
of *The Budget* and said to be an orator, who spoke on blacks in the
United States, and Mrs. Woods, an author. Dr. Love dealt with the inequalities of life in Jamaica. As if to contradict Olivier's claim that
blacks had equality of opportunity in Jamaica, he pointed out that no
black or colored man sat on a single government board or rose even to

a subinspectorship in the police force. The meeting passed a resolution to be sent to the British Parliament condemning the ill-treatment of the native people in South Africa.

Among the places Williams visited in the countryside was Porus, a town in Manchester Parish, forty-seven miles by rail west of Kingston. There he addressed a large audience in a Baptist chapel, and an association branch was formed with the pastor, the Rev. S. J. Washington, as chairman. Apart from dealing with the origins of the Pan-African movement, Williams pointed to the political, social, and economic disabilities of black Jamaicans with which he had become acquainted.

Williams's reception had been generally cordial except in Mandeville, not far from Porus, where his views were challenged by the schoolmaster of the Middle School, M. F. Johns. Williams reported to Love that Johns, in whose school the meeting had been held, had come armed with books to refute "incontestable facts" of current history, such as the existence of slavery under the British flag and the iniquities of the compound system in South Africa. Additionally, Johns claimed that even if what Williams said was true, this information should not be made public because it would lead to "insurrectionary acts" by our people."[13] Johns saw black contact with whites as beneficial to the former; Williams recognized that the aggressive, totalitarian nature of the European invasion tended to snuff out the traditions, customs, institutions, and values of Africans.[14] Williams wrote not long afterwards of Africans as "a distinct and peculiar people."[15] In a letter to the *Leader* he had maintained that African "customs, practices and rites" were different, and they should not be discarded but preserved. Africans had their own civilization, he wrote, and that of another people should not be forced on them against their will. In using the term "individuality" Williams was expressing the concept that Edward Blyden wrote of as the "African personality," only expressing it with a slightly different word. [16]

On May 3 the executive committee of the Jamaica branch of the Pan-African Association, at a farewell meeting held in Kingston, presented Williams with a surprise address complimenting him on the success of his mission. In returning thanks, Williams declared that blacks could no longer be ignored. Their sons and daughters could be seen in nearly every walk of progress, though he had observed that attempts were being made to limit their education and so impede their advance. The times demanded that they close ranks, and he could not accept the claim that the people of the West Indies could not unite; the Pan-African Association in Jamaica provided the opportunity to unite the islands, and he trusted they would use every moment to perfect the work. What he evidently had in mind was that they should work for race uplift in the Pan-African Association, responding to the cry of humanity on behalf of "their own kinsmen" in Africa and working at the same time for a federation of the British West Indian colonies. Williams later claimed that the "majority of people" believed that a federation was desirable. He advocated it on the score of economy and as a means of ensuring the impartial administration of justice.[17]

The desire on the part of Williams's friends to obtain the seal of official approval for a farewell concert in his honor gave Governor Hemming the opportunity to display the official hostility to the Pan-African movement. Because he considered it threatening to force the pace of change and so disrupt the white-dominated society, the governor rebuffed Williams and Mrs. McKenzie, the secretary of the Kingston branch of the association, when they called to ask his patronage for the fund-raising effort. The governor's patronage would have been a simple courtesy to respectable subjects, but Hemming was an upholder of the status quo who considered Love a "most dangerous" person, [18] Jamaicans generally "a beastly lot,"[19] and the Pan-African Association aggressive and disruptive. Williams delivered the feature address at the concert, which the lack of the governor's patronage and the want of a large attendance seemed not to make less enjoyable. Olivier had been expected but failed to appear; he could not act as if in disagreement with the governor. But some "well known faces" were noted, among them Campbell, Alleyne, and Dixon. Williams summed up the observations of a six-week visit on his return to the West Indies after ten years abroad. Accepting the conventional European view that equates illegitimacy with immorality, he called upon the people of Jamaica to wipe out immorality, which he blamed on bad housing conditions; there were too many one-roomed houses. And he lamented the prevailing low wages. As he would urge again on his countrymen in Trinidad, he called on Jamaicans to take advantage of educational opportunities and to do things for themselves instead of dreaming and talking. He said he had formed a favorable impression of the potential of Jamaica and its people. Altogether he considered his visit to Jamaica on behalf of the Pan-African Association a success. In fact there had been a hearty response for he had added five hundred members to the association's roll. It was a good start to his tour, which took him home to Trinidad.

Going home to Trinidad after an absence of ten years was a pleasant prospect for Williams. In his work for the Pan-African movement he already had stalwart supporters there. Maresse-Smith and the Rev. Mr. Douglin of the emancipation jubilee days were still there as were Lazare, who had been named vice-president of the association for Trinidad, Bass, and Phipps. Yet he was somewhat apprehensive about the kind of public reception his message would get. Unlike Jamaica, which had a very largely African-descended population, Trinidad's African dominance had been steadily whittled away by subsidized immigration from India. Despite continuing protest, this immigration was still being carried out under Chamberlain's policy of nullifying African numerical superiority in the Antilles. [20] While the Africans still formed the strongest grouping numerically, there was a sizable, growing Indian population, the bulk of which was still under indenture, bound to the sugar estates.

Williams arrived in Port-of-Spain on May 15, 1901. He received a "very warm welcome" the following day in his native Arouca, "hundreds of people turning out to shower good wishes on him." The women and girls kissed him as he went along, and he "visited the homes of almost every inhabitant of the neighborhood, from the most respectable dwelling to the peasant's humble cot." [21]

There was no newspaper in Port-of-Spain preaching black uplift like Dr. Love's *Jamaica Advocate* in Kingston. Except for *Creole Bitters,* a small humorous paper edited by H. S. Billouin, an old advocate of reform, the newspapers were owned or edited by white men. The liberal Englishman, R. R. Mole, whom Rostant had brought over as a shorthand writer for his *Public Opinion* in the 1880s, now owned and edited the *Mirror,* carrying on the old tradition. Joseph de la Sauvagère, Trinidad-born veteran of the Franco-Prussian war, edited the *Port-of-Spain Gazette.* Rostant was still alive, though at eighty-two he was out of both politics and journalism. There was to be no difficulty about fair publicity, and indeed there was enthusiastic support on Mole's part. Just as in earlier times, however, the absence of black men in the crown colony legislature remained an irritant to public-spirited men.

On the second day after his arrival the *Mirror* published a long question-and-answer interview, which ended with the only contemporary description of Williams. He was "of medium height, with massive head, heavy build and clear cut pleasant features." The interviewer, evidently a believer in the then-popular but now discredited phrenology, judged that his "forehead proclaimed him a man of intelligence" and he deduced from Williams's ready speech that he was no stranger to platform work and noted his very strong belief in "the destiny of his race." [22]

During the fortnight before his first meeting, Williams traveled to San Fernando, Princes Town, and other towns arranging meetings. His first public appearance had to be postponed because of the holidays. Apart from the Whitsun holiday there was Trinity Monday, which was observed in Diego Martin with "the Africans" holding fetes in different places and the schools being closed "for want of attendance." It was a people's holiday not sanctioned by authority. Williams spent this time arousing interest in the Pan-African Association, and there were "about one thousand persons, principally males," at the Princes' Building, Port-of-Spain, on the night of May 31 to hear Williams expound its aims and objects. Among the persons on the platform were Lazare, Maresse-Smith, Dr. Bass, Mrs. Philip John, wife of an art teacher and secretary of the association, and Samuel Cobham and Andrew McCarthy, solicitors. As convener, Lazare invited Maresse-Smith to take the chair after an introductory talk in which he recalled his meetings with Mrs. Kinloch at Chelsea Barracks during his visit to England and how the African Association came to be formed. [23]

Williams was warmly greeted by the audience. He was relaxed, and there was no Olivier to steal his thunder. In a long speech he reviewed the origin and work of the African and Pan-African associations and called for greater and more determined efforts to win full human rights for blacks in and out of the continent of Africa.

Williams, like any other English lawyer, believed in constitutional processes and advised that any measures they adopted must be constitutional because it was only under the Constitution, he explained, that wrongs could be righted. Blacks needed representatives in England through whom they could secure the genuine sympathy of the English people. These representatives would be able to counter the propaganda of Englishmen from the islands, who gave them a bad name. In that way and by making representations to Parliament, where there were men willing to assist their efforts, they would change the practice of refusing army commissions to West Indians in spite of their willingness to fight England's battles.

In replying to the vote of thanks moved by Maresse-Smith and passed unanimously, Williams restated the association's policy on black-white relations. The seconder, J. C. Cox, had warned that in upholding the rights of the race, they should not alienate those whites who had helped them. Williams noted that one of the aims of the association was to have friendly relations between African and European, but he emphasized, "We shall never be men until we learn to speak out about our rights as men."

During the month of June great enthusiasm was generated as Williams addressed meetings at Sangre Grande, San Fernando, Princes Town, Sainte Madeleine, Arima, Tunapuna, and Arouca. From places where meetings had not been scheduled, deputations or messages were sent inviting him to come, and the month of activities came to a climax on June 21 with another meeting at the Princes' Building.

At the meeting held at the Victoria Hall, San Fernando, over which Canon Douglin presided, there were among the "large and enthusiastic" audience "representatives of the most intelligent and better classes of the colored and black sections of the town and the Naparimas."[24] Canon Douglin was elected branch chairman and G. Ashton Warner, solicitor and a member of Maresse-Smith's emancipation jubilee deputation to the governor in 1888, secretary. As in San Fernando, at the Princes Town meeting there was a large audience, including "many ladies," and Grecian Donawa, a merchant interested in the plight of the neighboring cane farmers, was elected branch chairman.

In a year of general economic depression the sugar factories had left the bulk of the farmers' sugarcane on the ground, giving priority in milling to the produce of their own fields. The farmers were driven to call for the erection of a central factory, and Williams undertook to raise the question with the Colonial Office on his return to London. But short of raising capital on their own—a remote possibility—such a project was not likely to commend itself to the British government, whose first concern was the protection of the British sugar-planting interests rather than those of the Trinidadian cane farmer.

Williams spent June 22 to 24 in Arouca, attending service in the

Presbyterian church and holding a meeting in the government school. The room was packed "from corner to corner" with the "ladies in the majority" in a total of over five hundred persons including the "most influential persons of the African race" in Arouca.[25] Among those on the platform were C. W. Phipps, his son R. E. Phipps, Rev. Dickson, and H. A. Nurse, the brilliant and public-spirited headmaster of Tacarigua Anglican School. (Nurse was the father of George Padmore, the activist and historian of Pan-Africanism, whose name was originally Malcolm Nurse. Padmore is said to have claimed kinship with Williams but this is not confirmed though his father was said to have come from Arouca.)

In taking the chair at the invitation of Richard Phipps, Dickson expressed pride in the achievements of Williams, a "child of Arouca." Williams said he was glad to be back in his home village and among old friends. He specifically referred to the support that Richard Phipps had given him in London in the early, difficult days of the African Association.

On June 25 Williams went by invitation to Tunapuna to speak on "The Disabilities of the Negro Race in Africa," under the chairmanship of A. E. Valentine, a planter. In the audience were G. F. Peters, a bailiff, Phipps and Nurse, both of whom spoke, W. S. Codrington, headmaster of St. Joseph Anglican School, Mr. and Mrs. Philip John, J. Payne, and "a large number" of the men of I Company, Trinidad Light Infantry Volunteers, whose regular drill night it was and who came in full uniform.[26]

There was a large audience for the formal launching of the Trinidad branch of the Pan-African Association on June 28, 1901. On the platform were the representatives of the local branches in Naparima, Sangre Grande, Arima, Manzanilla, Tunapuna, Arouca, and Chaguanas. The others were Rt. Rev. James Thomas Hayes, Anglican bishop of Trinidad, Hon. H. C. Bourne, acting colonial secretary, Mrs. Bourne, Canon Douglin, Maresse-Smith, Lazare, his wife and her sister Miss Swoard, Mrs. Philip John, secretary, H. S. Billouin, and S. J. Robinson, a headmaster.

After moving Canon Douglin to the chair, Lazare read a letter from the governor, Sir Cornelius Alfred Moloney, whom he had invited to the meeting. Moloney regretted he could not attend but enclosed a donation to the association.[27] His attitude was in striking contrast to that of Governor Hemming in Jamaica, for he expressed his general sympathy with the association's objects. But in claiming that Africans and their descendants were not discriminated against and were taking high rank in legislatures, he was turning a blind eye to the Trinidad legislature where there were no blacks (he was to make the first appointment a few years later). There were also many posts in the civil service, including the police, to which no black man had yet risen.

Bishop Hayes, the main speaker, advised the members of the association to be ambitious, self-reliant, and morally strong. They should send representatives to Africa to teach these three principles to the natives. [28] Many new members were enrolled at the close of the meeting.

Williams's visit to Trinidad attracted attention in the neighboring islands, and his activities were reported and commented upon in the newspapers. Grenada sent a message asking for Williams to visit and establish a branch. [29] Shortly after the meeting Lazare announced a plan by "leaders of the movement" to send two representatives to the other West Indian islands to canvass the idea of holding a conference in Trinidad in six months' time. They would send congratulations to King Edward VII on his accession to the throne and seek from him the grant of "political freedom—a voice in the management of their own affairs." [30] But nothing came of this idea.

The time for Williams's departure was fast approaching. He addressed a meeting in Comparo and shortly afterward was entertained at a farewell dinner given by old teaching colleagues at the Standard Hotel, Port-of-Spain. It was not a temperance gathering for the toast to the king was drunk in champagne though the menu contained no reference to any other intoxicant. S. J. Robinson presided and the other diners included Lazare, T. H. Cross (Williams's former teacher), C. C. Smith, Sydney Smith, Cobham, and H. A. Nurse. Williams spoke of the need for black unity, emphasizing that the chances of a successful future for the Pan-African Association would be considerably enhanced by the support it received in the West Indies. [31]

On the eve of his sailing, Williams received a farewell address and purse from the people of Arouca and was a guest at a farewell reception by members of Faithful Brothers of Souls in Purgatory Friendly Society. The presentation was held in the government school. A deputation from the village branch of the Pan-African Association, including the Rev. Mr. Dickson, chairman, Richard Phipps, secretary, and Sydney Smith, treasurer, waited on him, and Dickson read the address in the presence of a number of villagers, including Williams's brother Hamilton. [32] Williams then left for Port-of-Spain. The Hall of Faithful Brothers in Upper Queen Street was crowded for the farewell reception. Among those seated at the horseshoe table were E. J. Ryan, president, M. A. Sylvester, secretary, H. S. Billouin, Alfred Richards, an Afro-Chinese druggist who later was president of the Trinidad Workingmen's Association, and Stephen Cobham, solicitor. Cobham, the principal speaker, expressed the hope that Williams would return with a charter of liberty from King Edward VII for all blacks in the British empire. [33]

The *Mirror* described Williams's two-month visit as a "great work." It found he had been "most conscientious, conspicuously fair" and that he had spoken with a "broad and high conception" of the duty he had voluntarily undertaken to perform. He had taken a high place in the public esteem, and if the cause should fail it would not be his fault. Blacks in the West Indies had needed a vigorous awakening to a full sense of their duty to themselves; they needed to be thrifty and to acquire a stake in the country. By their doing so, the *Mirror* declared, political power would come. [34]

Williams did not announce, as he had done in the case of Jamaica, how many members had been enrolled, but he was satisfied with the response. A significant feature of the campaign was the participation of men who, in earlier years, had been involved in manifestations of black consciousness. For example, the names reappear of a number of those who, as young men, were associated with Maresse-Smith in the emancipation jubilee controversy of 1888 or with an earlier presentation in 1885 of a silver purse of golden sovereigns to Maresse-Smith for his "manly courage" as a pamphleteer in exposing unsavory conditions in the administration of justice.

After Williams's departure for the United States new branches of the association were formed. The lively Couva branch sent a deputation to Claxton's Bay, at the request of the friendly societies there, to found a branch. The speeches there and elsewhere showed that the members were fully acquainted with Williams's ideas and with the origins and aims of the association. At meetings, subscriptions were received for the *Pan-African,* the monthly magazine that Williams planned to publish in London, and concerts were held to raise funds. Williams's visit, it appears, even inspired efforts at musical composition, for at a promenade concert given by the Couva branch on September 2 the branch's glee company presented, as its opening chorus, "Forward, Sons of Africa," described as "a West Indian composition," which was rendered for the first time in Trinidad and was well received. [35]

But there was a continuous cry for guidance, which Lazare, the vice-president, seemed unable or was too busy to give. The Couva branch was building up a library, which was housed in the home of Chairman James Headlie at Exchange Village, and among newspapers available was T. Thomas Fortune's *New York Age*. At Sangre Grande there were proposals for a syndicate with shares of one pound each, though the purpose was not disclosed. A similar suggestion was put forward at the Tunapuna branch with the idea of buying and working land, showing that the members were imbued with the spirit of black enterprise.

Williams had stressed two topics in addition to the franchise to his audiences. These were the importance of involving women in the activities of the association and the education of their children. He even seems to have suggested the co-opting of women when they failed to secure election to branch committees.

Williams's West Indian visit coincided with proposals by the Colonial Office to reduce expenditure on education although fees had been abolished in primary schools from the first of the year in Trinidad. Therefore, Williams supported Maresse-Smith and Lazare, who were the leading promoters of a petition against the abolition of government schools—a step that would have placed the control of education in the hands of the clergy. He advised that there was no agency better fitted than the state to oversee the education of children, so resolutions were passed at his meetings demanding the retention of government schools. His collaborators in the propagation of the pan-African idea were very often schoolmasters and they readily joined—even those of them employed in church schools—in opposing the turning over of the state schools to the churches.

To the company of teachers toasting him at the farewell dinner, Williams urged the necessity of training their pupils so they would be interested in the welfare of the country and so imbued with manly virtues that they would stand squarely together in their own cause. He linked this advice with condemnation of England's policy of denying political rights to West Indians.

By the time Williams returned to London in September, the petition had reached the Colonial Office, and he submitted his supporting views on education and other questions raised in Trinidad and Jamaica for Chamberlain's consideration. It was undesirable, he said in a memorandum, to do away with state schools because of the complex religious condition of the island where the Roman Catholic church and the Church of England were "fighting for the division of the spoils." [36] If education were placed wholly in the hands of the clergy, the "obvious result" would be confusion and greater expenditure of money. He advocated "more consideration" for teachers and the commissioning of an expert to report on education and expansion of the curriculum throughout the West Indies, instead of restricting it as planned.

After Williams left Trinidad for the United States, Vice-President Lazare became involved in other affairs apart from his law practice; letters appeared in the newspapers criticizing him for his lack of activity in the association. The Port-of-Spain branch had not met in two months, and the branches lacked dynamic leadership. Lazare took notice of early criticism by publishing in the newspapers questions asked in the House of Commons by Sir Charles Dilke at the request of the association about incidents in South Africa to show that the association, at least in London, was functioning. [37] But the Arouca branch, after waiting four months for a reply from Lazare to their letter complaining about the inactivity of the leadership, decided to communicate directly with Williams.

During his stay in Jamaica and Trinidad, Williams had kept Bishop Walters informed of the progress of his mission. He received in Trinidad a letter from the bishop in Indianapolis complimenting him on the "splendid" work done so far and asking him to convey his compliments to the different vice-presidents and the assurance that "the U. S. will welcome them with open arms" at a conference to be held in Boston in 1902, "according to the decision of our first conference in London last year." Walters said that he and the "members of the committee" awaited Williams in New York as arranged and asked when he planned to arrive. [38]

It is not clear which committee Walters had in mind—whether it was the American members of the committee of the Pan-African Association or the committee of the National Afro-American Council, which was preparing for its fourth annual meeting in Philadelphia on August 7, 8, and 9. If it was the former it would have meant that Du Bois, who was spending the summer with his family at Sea Island, New Jersey,[39] would join Walters in welcoming him; if the latter, it would have meant that among the party would be T. Thomas Fortune, editor of the *New York Age,* occasional collaborator of Booker T. Washington and self-styled "most distinguished pencil-pusher of the Afro-American fraternity," [40] for he was the chairman of the Afro-American Council's executive committee.[41] Fortune, a mulatto, became an editor of Marcus Garvey's publications toward the end of his life and found Garvey to be strictly honest.[42]

A meeting between Williams and Fortune would have been historic, for Fortune was to claim in 1906 in an article in the *New York Age,* "A Pan-African Congress," that he was the originator of the Pan-African idea while Williams was in New York but that Williams had "seized upon it" and later called the Pan-African Conference, which had not amounted to much. There is no record of Fortune's confronting Williams with a charge of "theft," and there is no evidence at all to support Fortune's claim. At the annual meeting of the Council, Williams met a wide cross-section of Afro-American leadership. Fortune took a prominent part in the meeting and was elected one of the vice-presidents while Williams himself delivered "an able address," "The Union of the Negro Races." At the banquet and reception held in the Odd Fellows' Temple, Fortune toasted "Negro Manhood" and Williams "The Pan-African Association." [43] Williams's presence was highlighted by the objection of a delegate to the spending of twenty-five dollars from the council's fund to defray his expenses in attending the meeting. [44]

At the end of his visit to the United States, Williams could look back with satisfaction on the results of nearly four years of dedicated voluntary work since the launching of the African Association. In the year that had elapsed since the conference, branches of the Pan-African Association had been set up in Jamaica and Trinidad. What Williams thought of the situation in the United States it is not possible to say but he may have been optimistic; the week after the meeting of the National Afro-American Council, the *Colored American* expressed the cautious opinion that the Pan-African Association "should secure a foothold in this country."[45]

NOTES

1. W. P. Livingstone, *Black Jamaica* (London: Sampson, Low, 1899), p. 139.

2. *Marylebone Mercury and West London Observer,* April 29, 1907. Barnard was known to this author in St. Lucia in the 1920s and 1930s as a landowner and nonpracticing barrister; he was among the first elected members of the Legislative Council.

3. H. A. Will, *Constitutional Change in the British West Indies, 1880-1903* (Oxford: Clarendon Press, 1970), p. 64.

4. Ibid., p. 271.

5. Ibid., p. 301.

6. *Jamaica Times,* November 28, 1914.

7. J. R. Love, *Is Dr. Holly Innocent?* (Port-au-Prince: T. M. Brown, 1883).

8. *Jamaica Advocate,* March 2, 1901.

9. Founded by Dr. Love as a forum to discuss problems of the black Jamaica masses, it met every year on August 1, Emancipation Day, in Spanish Town and passed resolutions to be sent to the Jamaican and British governments.

10. Livingstone, *Black Jamaica,* p. 152n.

11. Will, *Constitutional Change,* pp. 244-245.

12. *Pan-African* (October 1901): 4.

13. *Jamaica Advocate,* June 8, 1901.

14. Ibid., June 15, 1901.

15. *Pan-African,* October 1901, p.1.

16. See Hollis R. Lynch, *Edward Wilmot Blyden, Pan-Negro Patriot, 1832-1912* (London and New York: Oxford University Press, 1967), p. 61.

17. *Pan-African* (October 1901): 5.

18. Will, *Constitutional Change,* p. 271.

19. Ibid., p. 260.

20. Ibid., pp. 243-244.

21. *Mirror,* May 31, 1901.

22. Ibid., May 17, 1901.

23. Ibid., June 1, 1901; *Gazette,* June 2, 1901; *Daily News,* June 2, 1901.

24. *Daily News,* June 13, 1901.

25. Ibid., June 26, 1901.

26. *Daily News,* June 27, 1901.

27. *Port-of-Spain Gazette,* June 29, 1901. Moloney had formerly worked in the British colonial service for some fifteen years in West

Africa and as governor of Lagos in the late 1880s he was influenced
by the ideas of the great pan-Africanist Edward Wilmot Blyden; see
Lynch, *Edward Wilmot Blyden*, pp. 221, 224, 228.

28. *Port-of-Spain Gazette,* June 29, 1901.

29. *Daily News,* June 29, 1901.

30. *Mirror,* July 8, 1901.

31. Ibid., July 6, 1901.

32. Ibid., July 16, 1901.

33. Ibid., July 13, 1901.

34. Ibid., July 12, 1901.

35. Ibid., September 6, 1901.

36. *Pan-African* (October 1901): 5.

37. *Mirror,* September 4, 1901.

38. Ibid., July 6, 1901.

39. *Colored American,* June 29, 1901.

40. Ibid., August 10, 1901.

41. Ibid., June 22, 1901.

42. T. Thomas Fortune, "The Passing Show," in *Norfolk Journal and Guide,* December 12, 1927.

43. *Colored American,* August 17, 1901.

44. *North American,* August 10, 1901.

45. *Colored American,* August 17, 1901.

Coup d'Etat and Reconstruction

Throughout his journey Williams had been greatly concerned about events in London. When he was in Trinidad he had heard that within a month of his leaving headquarters, "certain colleagues" had dissolved the Pan-African Association "on the pretext of lack of funds" and announced it to the press.[1] Although deeply wounded by this "illegality,"[2] he had made no public announcement of the incident in Trinidad, but did write to Love, who made a brief announcement in his paper. Love assured his readers that the association would be resuscitated on Williams's return to London.[3] Williams discussed a plan of action with Bishop Walters who, by coincidence, was returning to London for the Ecumenical Congress of Methodism to be held there.

The Pan-African Association had been brought into existence with a debt of twenty-two pounds, the deficit on the conference. Williams's absence could hardly have paralyzed activities so quickly that this "unwarranted precipitancy" was called for, and he complained, with good cause, that this action had been taken without the knowledge of Walters or himself or other members of the executive committee not in London.[4] There was an element of back-stabbing about it, the cause of which went deeper than the mere lack of funds, as the subsequent course of the dissidents showed. It seems likely that it was Dr. Colenso, general treasurer of the Pan-African Association and the only executive officer in England during Williams's absence, who changed the name of the organization to the Anglo-African Association.[5] Like other British humanitarians Colenso no doubt thought that Williams and his black associates were too emphatic about black racial solidarity under black leadership.

Although Love's first reaction on hearing the news of the change of name of the organization from Williams had been to say "an enemy hath done this" and to describe the dissolution as having occurred in "very suspicious circumstances," he readily secured compliance by the Jamaica branches with Colenso's advice to adopt the "Anglo-African" title.[6] He was moved by "the unmistakable evidence of the fidelity and interest of the philanthropic gentlemen and ladies in England" who were prepared to act in concert with their African fellow subjects.[7]

In so doing Love was denying the pan-Africanism to which he had so readily adhered after meeting Williams. Given his intense loyalty to Britain in spite of his American training, it was not surprising that he was readily receptive to the change of name. He might already have been apprised of the proposals for change of name when he wrote:

> The Pan-African Association is an organization of British birth by British Negroes and should depend not on the Afro-American. Its headquarters must be in England, and its controlling influence must be British. As only through British authority can the Pan-African Association achieve its high aims.[8]

Here was the race-conscious Love putting nationality before race. He was indeed objecting to Walters's leadership on the ground of his being American and narrowing to national limits the scope of an organization that was intended to have international dimensions. He apparently thought that there should have been a counterpart British organization to the National Afro-American Council, working for British Negroes, but he was dismissing the idea of cooperation and mutual help among Afro-British, Afro-Americans, and Africans. It may be that a different organizational structure was needed—national associations affiliated to and represented on a central international body—but the remedy was not a break with the Afro-Americans and dissolution of the Pan-African Association.

In the meantime, obviously unaware of the goings-on between Jamaica and London, Williams had arrived in London on September 4 with Bishop Walters. After a meeting with members of the association on September 13, they announced that the Pan-African Association would continue and that the members elected to the executive committee at the conference were "considered to have resigned" and other persons had been appointed in their stead.[9] The announcement said that Williams was to continue as general secretary until the 1902 conference in the United States.

The appointees to the executive committee were "Bishop Small

(Penn.), Dr. R. N. [*sic*] Love (Jamaica), Lieut. Lazare (Trinidad),
Henry Smith, Esq. (London), Tengo Jabavu (S. A.), J. Otonba Payne,
Esq. (Lagos)." [10] Only Rev. Henry Smith among these had been at
the Pan-African Conference, and his address was given as London, England,
in Walters's list of delegates. Nothing is known about him but, like
the other appointees, he must have been black. Bishop Small, Walters's
colleague on the board of bishops of the AME Zion church, is described
by Harold R. Isaacs as "Bishop John Bryant Small, a West Indian who had
been a soldier in the British Army and then become a missionary in
Africa."[11] Walters eulogized him as a "sainted Hero . . . eminent scholar."
and "enthusiastic advocate of African redemption." [12]

It does not appear that the reconstituted committee ever functioned
though Williams must have notified the overseas members of their appointment and kept them informed of his activities. Love's appointment
would have been an abortive act. Neither Williams nor Walters knew at
the time that he was already on the other side. Unfortunately it is not
possible to pursue the fate of the Anglo-African Association. There is
no evidence that it functioned in Jamaica, or in Trinidad where the Pan-
African Association branches were in operation until the middle of 1902.

Williams's main concern on his return to London was the revival of
the Pan-African Association, but before the meeting he had sought and
failed to get an interview with Chamberlain to bring to his attention
conditions in the West Indies. The assistant under-secretary, C. P. Lucas,
wrote asking him to submit a memorandum instead. This he did, raising
preeminently the question of the franchise in Trinidad. He reported a
general dissatisfaction because of the lack of representation and proposed a property qualification of twenty pounds annual ratable value.
He claimed to be speaking on behalf of "a large portion of the people
of Trinidad and Jamaica . . . educated, thinking men and women . . . land
and house owners, merchants, artisans, and so on." [13]

Williams also called for agricultural banks to help Jamaica's peasant
proprietors who experienced "indescribable hardships" for want of
credit, central factories to grind the cane of Trinidad's cane farmers, and
a federation of the West Indies, which he said a majority of the people
desired. There was not even a reply to Williams's plea.

Williams was conscious of the importance of publicity for enlightening whites and for exposing racial inequities. He also knew that there were few vehicles for blacks to use to express their grievances. They had no representatives in the British Parliament, nor did they own a news- paper. To remedy this situation, Williams published in October 1901 the first issue of *The Pan-African*. The journal was a monthly paper de- signed to diffuse information "concerning the interests of the African and descendants in the British Empire." [14] This might appear to be a reverting to the position of the "Anglo-Africans," but this stance was probably adopted merely for convenience and was not an abandonment of the Pan-African idea.

Williams is listed as editor, but while one contemporary reviewer speaks of the paper as having been founded "to support the movement recently inaugurated by the Pan-African Association," [15] there is nothing to indicate that it was the organ of the association. In fact, the first issue contains only three short items relating to the association and the only reference to ownership is one to unidentified "proprietors" in the imprint at the foot of the back cover. It seems, however, that by January 1902 the journal had been turned into a limited liability com- pany of five hundred one-pound shares, which suggests that it had been a private venture that Williams promoted.[16]

The introductory editorial justified the venture by asserting that "in the face of insufficient representation" the one way that "the unfortunates inhabiting the territories of the British Empire" could express their feelings was through "an humble newspaper." The editorial ended on a note that was a persistent theme with Williams: "We are convinced that no other but a Negro can represent a Negro."[17] Williams seemed to look upon himself as destined for the task, for he added that "the times demand the presence of that Negro to serve the cause of a people the most despised and ill-used today."

The journal received friendly reviews in London and Trinidad. A reviewer in the socialist weekly *Reynolds's* thought there was no gentleman more qualified for the post of editor than Williams, "from what I have observed of his public career." The Liberal *Star* said that, in order to "undeceive" their fellow citizens of the empire, Williams and his friends had had recourse to establish a newspaper wholly given over to pleading the cause of "the poor African and the amelioration of his lot."[18] The tone of these reviews and the en- couraging and sympathetic message from his friend, James Keir Hardie,

Labour MP, which the paper carried, shows that Williams was well known in socialist circles.

In Trinidad the *Mirror* published a long review in which it recalled the help it gave to the movement during Williams's visit and observed that "the claims of the British Negro are put forward in an able, just and reasonable manner," which had already done much "to gain the respect of the other race in Trinidad" for the Pan-African Association.[19]

The history of the *Pan-African* is obscure, and in fact only the first issue—one copy in the British Museum—survives. There were certainly more issues of the *Pan-African* and possibly six in all. The *Mirror* review of the November issue showed that while the magazine was designed to propagate the cause of the British African it did not neglect that of the Afro-American. One article dealt with the negative southern reaction to President Theodore Roosevelt's reception of Booker T. Washington at the White House. Mr. Washington, it asserted, was good enough to be received by any head of state.[20] Another article, "A Terrible Calamity in American History" by Professor W. S. Scarborough, was listed but its content was not indicated. The December issue carried articles on the call for reform in Trinidad, "The Maroons in Jamaica" and "Governor Eyre of Jamaica."[21]

In February 1902, it was announced in Trinidad that Edgar McCarthy, a printer, had been appointed local agent.[22] In mid-March Williams's brother Hamilton announced the magazine had been "somewhat delayed this month" as a result of the editor's being "laid up with influenza."[23] One month later he had on hand "the back numbers" and this was the last heard of it.[24]

Williams probably continued to give public lectures while working on the *Pan-African* and preparing for his postponed call to the bar. The one lecture on record in this period took him to Stoke, near Ipswich, on December 9, 1901, to speak to the Bridge Ward Liberal Club.[25] He spoke in "fluent, forcible fashion," only here and there betraying "a trace of accent." The topic was "Is the Negro a Factor in the British Empire?" which he appears to have developed into a booklet, *The British Negro: A Factor in Empire,* published in 1902.[26] In this lecture Williams disclosed that, like other black Britishers who had volunteered for service in the British forces in South Africa, he had been rejected on the grounds of color. In thus volunteering to fight in what his friend Keir Hardie was opposing and denouncing as a capitalist war, [27] Williams had accepted readily Lord Salisbury's statement in Guildhall in November 1899 that the treatment of the Africans by the Boers was one of the principal causes of the war and expected the situation to be remedied following a British victory.[28] From his later experience he would have regarded himself and others who thought like him as having been duped. Among these would have been F. J. Loudin, his Afro-American colleague at the conference, who wrote John E. Bruce urging that prominent Afro-Americans write to the British ambassador in Washington expressing confidence in British rule in South Africa.[29]

Williams told the white Liberal audience that all of Britain's West African possessions were acquired by "the valor of our black soldiers," referring no doubt to the roles of West African forces and the West India Regiment. In spite of the British declaration that Africans would not be used as soldiers in South Africa, Williams said they had in fact been used. They were defenders of the empire in time of war and consumers of "home produce" in time of peace, and yet they were denied basic rights.

In the West Indies blacks were heavily taxed while denied the vote, and in South Africa they were in a state of "practical slavery." The African, he declared, was not being enlightened; he was being degraded and demoralized under imperial rule.

It must have been in 1902 that the last was heard of the Pan-African Association. Organizations formed by colonials in a metropolitan capital tend to fluctuate in strength and activity with the ebb and flow of residents. The people from the West Indies and Africa from whom the organization would have drawn its working membership were not numerous. Williams claimed fifty working members in England during his visit to Trinidad. [30] Few of them lived there permanently; they were mainly students, most of whom invariably left for home after their studies. Moreover, few students join crusading organizations or assume, like Williams, the role of an activist.

It was probably in May 1902 that Williams decided that it was time to start practicing law, but he did not have the fees required for a formal call to the bar. In his search for financial assistance, Williams approached Dr. Greville Walpole, the chairman of the National Thrift

Society, for which he had lectured on thrift. Walpole, possibly unable to help personally, called the attention of the president of the
Anti-Slavery Society to a "most deserving case," [31] but the society
too was unable to help because it had "no funds." [32]

Williams evidently had made alternative arrangements, for on
June 11 he was among seventeen new barristers called by Gray's Inn.
Williams and Christian were the only West Indians among them and
also were among only six who did not have university degrees. [33] Not
long afterward, during the Trinity Sittings of the Court, Williams
signed the roll of barristers of the High Court of Justice, King's Bench
Division, at the Royal Courts of Justice admitting him to practice at
the English bar.

In deciding to practice in England, Williams probably became the
first black man to do so.

English barristers generally did not attain any conspicuous success
in the early years of practice. They supplemented their meager in-
comes by journalism or lecturing, at which Williams was adept, and
unless they had legacies, were maintained by relatives or had private
means. For a black man with a wife and two children after the turn
of the century it must have been difficult indeed in an alien environment where his living depended on white solicitors acting for white
clients.

Before a new barrister began his practice it was the custom for him
to serve a term of pupilage in the chambers of a practicing barrister.
Williams entered the chambers of Edgar Swan, staying there until the
following year when he went to South Africa. The extent or the nature
of his practice during this period is obscure but the records show that
two complaints were lodged against him with the benchers of Gray's
Inn by disgruntled clients. They were evidently of a trivial nature. In
one case the benchers decided there was not sufficient evidence to
justify the holding of an enquiry and in the other, "no order was made
out." [34]

The existence of the empire afforded a widened field of action
for the inhabitants of any of its component parts who had the urge
and the opportunity to travel. Fellow West Indians before him had
visited and worked in various parts of Africa as missionaries, teachers,
newspaper editors, traders, soldiers, sailors, and adventurers. [35] In
going to South Africa Williams was claiming what he would have des-

cribed as his civis Britannicus sum. He was a Britisher, a black barrister qualified to practice in England, and by the fact entitled to practice wherever the British flag flew.

While 1902 marks the end of Williams's connection with a formal Pan-African organization, his subsequent life provides ample proof that the Pan-African goal of black freedom, dignity, and integrity continued to be the major motivating force in his life.

NOTES

1. *Jamaica Advocate,* September 28, 1901.
2. *Pan-African* (October 1901): 4.
3. *Jamaica Advocate,* September 28, 1901.
4. *Pan-African* (October 1901): 4.
5. *Jamaica Advocate,* September 28, 1901.
6. Ibid., July 6, 1901.
7. Ibid., September 28, 1901.
8. Ibid., August 31, 1901.
9. *Pan-African* (October 1901): 4.
10. Ibid.
11. Harold R. Isaacs, *New World of Negro Americans* (New York: Viking Press, 1964), p. 129.
12. Alexander Walters, *My Life and Work* (New York: Fleming H. Revell Company, 1917), pp. 174-175. Jean Price-Mars, in *Silhouettes de Nègres et de Négrophiles* (Paris: Présence Africaine, 1960), p. 101, says that Small, in 1898, sent J. E. K. Aggrey and other young Africans from the Gold Coast to Livingstone College, North Carolina, for training as missionaries. Aggrey was to become widely known as an educator and advocate of black-white cooperation.
13. *Pan-African* (October 1901): 5.
14. Ibid., 4.
15. *Mirror,* December 2, 1901.
16. Ibid., February 23, 1902.
17. Cf. Blyden, "No people can interpret Africans but Africans," cited by George Shepperson, "Notes on American Influences on the Emergence of African Nationalism," *Journal of African History* 1 (1960): 299. Also, cf. Marcus Garvey, "Who best can interpret the anguish and needs of our people but a Negro?" A. J. Garvey, *Garvey and Garveyism* (New York: Collier Books, 1970), p. 26.

18. *Mirror,* December 11, 1901.
19. Ibid., December 2, 1901.
20. Ibid., December 16, 1901.
21. Ibid., January 25, 1902. The Maroons were courageous blacks who defied British slavery and control to set up their own society in the mountains of Jamaica; Edward Eyre achieved notoriety when, as governor of Jamaica, he suppressed with extreme brutality a black uprising in October 1865.
22. Ibid., February 22, 1902.
23. Ibid., March 13, 1902.
24. Ibid., April 14, 1902.
25. Ibid., January 8, 1902.
26. The author was unable to locate a copy.
27. A. J. P. Taylor, *The Trouble Makers* (London: Hamish Hamilton, 1957), pp. 91, 95.
28. *Jamaica Advocate,* March 2, 1901 (letter from Williams).
29. Loudin to Bruce, April 29, 1900, John H. Bruce Papers, Schomburg Collection, New York Public Library.
30. *Mirror,* June 1, 1901.
31. Walpole to Anti-Slavery Society, May 13, 1902, Anti-Slavery Papers, Rhodes House Library, Oxford.
32. Minute 1122 of Committee Meeting of the Anti-Slavery Society, June 6, 1902, Anti-Slavery Papers.
33. B. M. Cocks, Librarian, Gray's Inn, to the author, n.d. See also *Times,* June 12, 1902.
34. P. C. Beddingham, Library, Gray's Inn, to the author, July 2, 1970.
35. See Abioseh Nicol, "West Indians in West Africa," *Sierra Leone Studies* (June 1960): 14-23.

Race Work in   8
South Africa, 1903-1905

Williams's decision to go to South Africa to practice law must have
been made on the urging of friends there; perhaps Rawson Walter
Wooding was among them. Wooding, who came from British Guiana
(now Guyana) and had lived in London, was a teacher and accomplished musician who had migrated to South Africa and opened a private
school in Cape Town for colored children in June 1902.[1] In later
years he also ran a colored amateur musical society but eventually
migrated to the United States.[2] Other friends were John Tengo Jabauvu,
whom Williams had met in London in 1899 and with whom he later
corresponded, and Mrs. Kinloch from Natal, who had inspired him to
take an active interest in African problems and to form the African
Association.

When he was in Trinidad in 1901, Williams had spoken of the indig-
nity accorded a medical friend of his in South Africa: he had to observe the curfew for Coloreds and Africans. Thus, he was well aware
that the social climate in South Africa would be hostile to him. It
seems that as general secretary of the Pan-African Association he had
planned to visit South Africa,[3] but this appears to have been frustrated
by the war there and then by the failure of the Pan-African Association.
But the treaty ending the war was signed at Vereeniging on May 31,
1902, just before Williams was called to the bar. By that time he decided
to settle in South Africa and practice his profession, a bold step under
the circumstances. No nonwhite in South Africa was an attorney or
advocate, even in liberal Cape Colony where white domination, race
discrimination, and denial of rights to blacks were relatively milder than
in the other three colonies. This knowledge may even have spurred him
on to be the first.

It is not surprising, therefore, that on his arrival in Cape Town in

October 1903 Williams ran into difficulties, the nature of which can only be guessed at. He wrote about them in his first letter home to his wife—a letter that has been lost—and merely referred to them in passing in the second—"the difficulties one had to encounter." [4] Some of these difficulties concerned his admission to practice as an advocate of the High Court of the Cape of Good Hope, [5] for although he possessed the requisite qualifications, being of African descent he was classed among the colored.

The Cape Law Society, whose members later boycotted him, [6] may have raised objections to his admission as had been offered in the case of the Indian Mohandas K. Gandhi (later famous as Mahatma Gandhi) in Natal in 1893. To admit a nonwhite lawyer was to threaten white predominance. The Natal Law Society had said in Gandhi's case that when the regulations regarding admission of advocates were made, the possibility of a colored man applying could not have been contemplated. It had also questioned the authenticity of Gandhi's certificate. But the chief justice of Natal had ruled that the law made no distinction based on color. The court, he said, had no authority to prevent Gandhi from being enrolled as an advocate. [7]

In like manner, the obstacles placed in Williams's way—possibly before the matter came into court—would have been thrust aside by the Cape chief justice. Williams was fortunate that the justice was Sir Henry de Villiers. De Villiers was opposed to the color bar in the grant of the franchise, but he was in favor of a franchise so high that it would exclude all except the most industrious non-Europeans even though some whites also would fail to qualify. As chief justice he had strongly advocated, without success, reciprocity between the bars of the four colonies and those of the United Kingdom, Germany, and Holland. Yet he could hardly have conceived the possibility, until Williams came on the scene, that a black member of the English bar would put his views to the test. Faced squarely with the problem, he could not do otherwise than approve, for Williams's qualification was the same as his own (he had been called to the English bar in 1865). [8]

Because of De Villiers's decision Williams displayed his portrait in his chambers, though he would have been mistaken to have thought it an act of Afrikaner liberalism rather than merely one of conceding his legal rights. Williams was admitted on October 29, 1903. That day marked as well a break-through for the Africans and colored in

Cape Colony and the rest of South Africa: his petition for enrollment was granted in open court on the motion of Morgan Evans, and he was issued a certificate of admission to the Cape Bar after paying a fee of twenty pounds and signing the roll of advocates. [9]

The white English-language newspapers, *Cape Times* and *Cape Argus*, both took note of the event. The admission of a black man to practice as an advocate must have been a major topic of conversation in home and club, shop and tavern, farm and mission station, church hall and army mess. The Africans and colored would have been pleasantly surprised and made wry comments, the whites perturbed by this advance of the "Ethiopianism" that they dreaded but had difficulty in defining. Williams's future course of action—his practical interest in the education of African and colored children, his defense of nonwhite people in the courts, his advocacy of equal rights and of participation of all in politics—could fit into the vague concept in the European mind of so-called Ethiopianism, which they thought threatened white domination.

Abe Bailey, the gold magnate, defined succinctly in an Empire Day speech in Johannesburg in 1905 the "Ethiopian movement": "one under the guise of religion to instill in the minds of natives doctrines of equality with whites, also that South Africa was their country, and that they should regain it." [10] The origin of the name derives from the Bible. Many black preachers and even some leaders (Marcus Garvey, for example) held that a verse in the Psalms had specifically referred to the future of the black people. Thus, in a speech delivered in New York on January 1, 1922, commemorating President Lincoln's emancipation proclamation, Garvey said, "We must believe that the Psalmist had great hopes for this race of ours when he prophesied 'Princes shall come out of Egypt and Ethiopia shall stretch forth her hands unto God.' " [11] To many black Christians who interpret the Bible literally, the verse has been a source of solace in times of stress. In South Africa they would have leaned upon it for hope to be rid some day of their oppression.

An Ethiopian church had been founded on November 2, 1892, by the Rev. M. M. Mokone, of Pretoria, Transvaal, who had been an elder of the Wesleyan Methodist church. According to him, the concept dated back to 1886, the last year that the white and black Wesleyan ministers had met together in their district meetings. In that year the color line was drawn; white and black were required to meet separately, but the blacks were under a white chairman with a white secretary. [12]

The formation of an Ethiopian church did not mean that blacks severed their relations with white ministers; when the first Ethiopian church building was formally opened on November 5, 1893, in the Marabastad native location, the dedication sermon was preached by a white Methodist minister. Earlier that year the Ethiopian church had been recognized by the Transvaal government, but in 1896 it became amalgamated with the African Methodist Episcopal church of the United States and in March 1898 the militant AME bishop, Henry McNeal Turner, visited. The AME church attracted widespread attention because of its repudiation of white leadership and its American connections. There were breakaways from European missions, some of whom joined the AME or formed their own churches. Whites labeled all these Ethiopian and transformed them in their imagination into a dangerous organized movement dedicated to black supremacy.

The fear engendered in the Europeans may be exemplified in the evidence given by the Scottish medical missionary, Rev. Dr. James Stewart, of the Lovedale Mission, before the South African Native Affairs Commission on November 3, 1904. Stewart, described by a French missionary, the Rev. E. Jacottet, as "first among the best and most devoted friends and benefactors of the natives," [13] was alarmed that "the idea of 'equality,' " which had long been in the African mind, was then "growing too strongly." He called the Ethiopian movement "a revolt on the part of a certain number of Native ministers of various missions or denominations against white control ecclesiastically," and he thought that whether they sprang from Wesleyanism or Presbyterianism or any other source, they were all definitely antiwhite. Stewart was also disturbed by the tendency among Africans to go to the United States for education that was not available to them in South Africa and to bring back "wrong ideas, political and social." The education question, he told the commissioners, "runs into the Ethiopian question, and . . . the Ethiopian question runs into another question wider still." Stewart described this third question as "the political contour or shape that things may take shortly," which he thought "runs in their heads." It was "hazy, like unfocussed pictures in a magic lantern, at first, but it will come out more fully and more clearly bye-and-bye." [14] Stewart at one point used the term

"Mzimbaism" as an alternative for "Ethiopianism," from the name
of a minister of the Ethiopian church who, according to Stewart,
collected funds from his congregation and took ten boys to the United
States for education at Tuskegee. [15]

In effect, what Stewart was saying was that any effort by an African
to raise himself by education to the same level as whites was dangerous. In this context, Williams, the first black lawyer, was a bad example
to the Africans. He was infringing upon the privileges of the white man
by doing white man's work. The duty of the black man in South Africa,
according to Maurice S. Evans, was "to plough, to dig, to hoe, to fetch
and carry, to cook—all laborious and menial toil." [16]

Williams secured chambers in Cape Town in a building that also
housed the offices of the short-lived weekly *Spectator*, edited by
F. Z. S. Peregrino. [17] As editor of the *Buffalo Spectator*, Buffalo,
N.Y., Peregrino had been among more than one hundred signatories
to Bishop Walters's request to Fortune, as president of the National
Afro-American League, to call a meeting of black leaders in 1898.[18]
Peregrino was probably a West African who had arrived in South
Africa after living many years in England and the United States. [19] By
mid-November Williams had moved to another building, where he had
two large rooms occupied by his two clerks, linked by a flight of steps
leading to his smaller sanctum. [20]

In his second letter home, Williams told "Dearest Agnes" he could
not write at length because he was working on "two heavy briefs,"
marked twenty-five pounds each, for forgery and poisoning. "The
whole of South Africa" was looking upon him, and he must see that
"my debut in the criminal arena" would be "memorable." He wished
he were back in London again, but because there seemed a chance for
him to make "a little cash," he would "abide the flow of time." Then
he added, somewhat pathetically, to dear "Scout" [Mrs. Williams],
"At present it is very hard."[21]

Williams appeared at the Cape Town December sessions in defense
of a colored licensed wagon driver accused with four whites of theft
of tarpaulins from the army ordnance stores at Woodstock. His defense
that his client had merely acted as a carrier and was not an accomplice
was not accepted by the jury. Two of the accused were discharged
while the principal accused—a metal merchant—and his fourteen-year-old
son and Williams's client were found guilty. The boy was ordered to

receive fourteen lashes of the cane, his father was sentenced to such labor as he might be found capable of doing for a period of three years, and Williams's client was given nine months at hard labor.[22] The judge did not indicate why the white metal merchant could not endure the same hard labor as the colored wagon driver whom he had engaged.

The spotlight soon was turned upon Williams with greater intensity than before. On Christmas Eve the newspapers reported that there had been a shooting affray in his chambers the previous day. A black American cartage contractor had shot his reputed wife and Williams's West Indian chief clerk, Francis Augustus Egerton, in what appeared to be a love triangle. Williams himself had been in the inner office, separated by a light calico screen. The woman died in hospital two weeks later. Williams had come out of his office on hearing the explosions, seen the bleeding Egerton, and gone in pursuit of his assailant whom he saw being arrested by a policeman.[23]

The newspaper reports made Williams even better known. His practice took him to both the criminal and divorce courts in cases between nonwhite parties, but his presence at the bar was not welcomed by the majority of his white colleagues, who maintained a boycott against him and kept him out of the circuit and bar messes.[24] This, however, did not daunt him, for he relished his position as a trailblazer and was soon involved in community activities.

About this time the governor, Sir Walter Hely-Hutchinson, was lamenting the state of education among white children, 64 percent of whom, he said, went out into the world with their mental equipment totally undeveloped and useless for intellectual occupations or skilled work.[25] The situation was far worse among the deprived nonwhite children of Cape Colony, whom the governor did not mention in his address to the legislature. But in the absence of equal educational opportunity for their children, the leaders of the Cape colored made their own provision to counter this official discrimination by improving Wooding's Private Preparatory School.

The prospectus, issued in January 1904, said the school was "under the auspices of a Board of Managers" and had been improved to provide "a better system of Education" than was offered in the state schools.[26] It must have taken little persuasion for Williams to accept membership on the board. Teaching was his first love and, believing as he did that education made all the difference in the character of a people, he wished to do his part in his community. Among the subjects taught, according to the syllabus, were English history and South African history, and the prospectus named the members of the board: "J. M. Wilson, J. H. M. Gool, A. Abdurahman, M. B., H. Sylvester Williams, ADVCT., and J. W. Boyce, Secretary." These five were to work together in fields other than education affecting the rights of coloreds. Wilson and Boyce have never been identified, but Gool was a leader in the Indian Association while Dr. Abdullah Abdurahman was a Cape Malay medical practitioner who had qualified in Scotland. Abdurahman was to become an important figure on the South African political scene, and it was said that at a certain time his name was overshadowed only by that of Gandhi.[27]

In addition to the subject of education, the small group who formed the school board considered jury service by colored men an important issue. When trial by jury was first introduced in Cape Colony early in the nineteenth century, no distinction was made among inhabitants on the ground of race or color; the law, it was said, was colorblind. [28] Yet a dark face was seldom seen on a jury panel, and a nonwhite on trial for a serious crime found himself before a European judge, a jury of whites, a white prosecuting counsel, and, if he had the money to pay a lawyer, white counsel defending him, even though he lived in a country in which whites were a small minority of the population.

In February 1904, Williams led a deputation to Cape Attorney-General T. L. Graham to put to him the grievances nonwhites had on trial by jury. Williams's four school board colleagues were all in the deputation along with Peregrino, F. Gow (who may have been the Rev. F. M. Gow of the AME church), and W. Collins.[29] Collins had been the first president of the African Political Organization, the first colored group with membership in all four colonies of South Africa. It had been formed in 1902 in anticipation of the union of the Cape and Natal with Transvaal and Orange Free State. Established three years after Cecil Rhodes, the Cape premier, had promised "equal rights for every civilized man South of the Zambezi," its aims were "to promote unity between the colored races of South Africa and to obtain higher education for our children."[30]

Graham was a member of the House of Assembly and, being in liberal Cape Colony, dependent to a certain extent on colored votes. His attitude to the delegation was a mixture of affability and condescension, but he promised to see that more colored men were put on juries. There is no indication that anything came of his assurances.

Additionally, Williams and his school board colleagues were involved in a well-attended "mass meeting of colored people" in March 1904 to "protest against the treatment of Colored People in the Transvaal,"[31] who were reduced to second-class citizenship under the law. Among their grievances was their inability to hold property in their own names; it was held in trust for them by the government without whose permission they could not sell or transfer. They could not enter the general post office in Johannesburg but had to use a separate post office. They had to carry a pass to be shown to the police on demand and a permit costing one pound a year, which entitled them to use the sidewalk without molestation. They were denied the municipal franchise and barred from the public parks and the Wanderers cricket ground. There were inequalities in the separate laws relating to marriage. Furthemore, while interracial marriages were illegal, a white man could live with a colored woman, but if a colored man lived with a white woman they became subject to the Immorality Act.[32]

The flyer advertising the meeting read:

Colored Men, you are in danger in South Africa
Roll up, and speak your mind.
Speakers: J. Tobin, Dr. Abdurahman
Advocate Williams. [33]

John Tobin was a licensed "general dealer" in Cape Town who was also organizer and manager of a concert group, Tobin's Minstrels. He had succeeded in 1904 to the presidency of the African Political Organization.[34] His tenure as president of the APO was shortlived. An advocate of conciliation between colored and Afrikaner, he favored the South African party and had canvassed for it in the February 1904 Cape parliamentary elections, while his predecessor in office, Collins, had supported the Progressives. Two months later the Paarl branch of the APO passed a vote of no confidence in Tobin, and he was expelled from the organization. Abdurahman became president in 1905.

Williams was also chosen to preside at the meeting. It was a signal honor, a mark of confidence in a newcomer hardly six months in the community, but events had conspired to make him widely known and

to push him to the forefront among the colored people. The five
school board members were on the platform, evidencing their position
of leadership and their solidarity in the colored interest. The presence
of J. Bigaro of Paarl and H. M. Dollie, Abdurahman's uncle from
London, shows the great interest the meeting aroused in Cape colored
communities outside Cape Town. Women were also interested and involved; on the platform were Mrs. Tobin and Mrs. Abdurahman. Also
on the platform was Matt J. Fredericks, APO general secretary who
was to be the editor of its weekly organ, *A. P. O.* Hundreds remained
outside throughout the meeting, unable to gain admittance; the hall
was filled well before the start. [35]

There are no references to the sponsors of the meeting either in the
newspaper reports or on the flyer announcing it. If there was a sponsor-
ing organization it may have been considered politic not to mention
its name. There were other colored organizations in existence in addition
to the APO; Williams is said to have proposed that they combine their
operations. [36] From this and from the fact of his presiding, it may be
conjectured that it was his idea that such a meeting should be held.

In his brief speech introducing Abdurahman, Williams referred to
the meeting as "unique" and expressed his pride that so many nonwhites could get together as Britishers to express and seek redress of
their grievances. Abdurahman recalled the disabilities still being suffered by the Cape colored in the former Boer republics, now Orange River
Colony and Transvaal. These made hollow the phrase "equal rights
to all civilized men south of the Zambezi." Instead of the Cape's
liberal tradition spreading north they now feared the extension of the
vicious policy of Transvaal to the Cape. Abdurahman complained that
the nonwhites had endured their trials in the war in the belief that all
the rights of British subjects would be extended to them. Little did
they dream that their disabilities would be renewed under the British
flag. In the terms of peace the clause declaring that the legal rights of the
colored people would be the same as in Cape Colony had been deleted
and their rights discarded.

In spite of this gross betrayal, Abdurahman's confidence in Britain
remained undiminished; he did not believe, he declared, that many
people in England knew of the harsh and "un-British treatment" that
was meted out to them in the Transvaal. He therefore proposed a resolution declaring that the treatment of colored British subjects in the

Transvaal was now worse than they had endured under the Boer government. It asked the high commissioner to accord them "the rights and privileges which every race has the right to enjoy" and thus relieve them from a "wicked oppression." It was in vain that Abdurahman asked the Transvaal authorities to act "according to British traditions and fundamental truths."

In seconding Abdurahman's resolution, Tobin dismissed as unfounded the blame he said was attached to black Americans in the Cape Colony for so-called Ethiopianism. He called on the colored people to raise a unanimous outcry over their grievances and to send a delegation to England to protest against their treatment and against the importation of Chinese labor for the mines.

Williams, who spoke after vacating the chair to Wilson, agreed with Tobin's suggestion that they should send someone to England to advocate their cause, something he himself had earlier sought to do. He stressed the need for group unity and loyalty and also for sound and relevant education. The meeting passed a resolution calling for the drafting of a petition setting forth their "special grievances" to be sent to the king, the Transvaal authorities, and the British and South African Parliaments. [37]

Williams's must have been an effective speech; he left no doubt in the minds of his colored hearers that his sympathies were wholly with them. The impact of the meeting itself seemed to have been tremendous. The *Cape Times* allocated two and a half columns to this "largest gathering of colored people." Williams had spoken of equality, the word and the idea that Rev. Dr. Stewart was to condemn eight months later as a sure sign of Ethiopianism. By a coincidence, simultaneously with the colored meeting was a conference in Johannesburg of the white vigilance group, the Rand Pioneers; the latter called for more severe laws to deal with alleged assaults by Africans and colored upon white women. The penalties sought ranged from compelling all nonwhites to wear a distinctive badge to flogging and the death penalty.

The same issue of the *Cape Times Weekly* that reported these meetings carried on another page the lengthy report of the trial of the black American, McVicer, for murder, including the evidence of Williams and his clerk Egerton for the prosecution. McVicer was found guilty by the jury and sentenced to death by hanging. The trial report occupied the lower half of a page; the upper half was devoted to

a large cartoon, "An Angel of Peace," showing the face of an old
bearded white man with wings, bare feet, a sword inscribed "W. T.
Stead" in his left hand, and his right hand holding to his lips a
trumpet from which issued "Race Hatred, Treason, Rebellion." The
London editor, who was visiting South Africa, had hurled at his
head by the English-speaking press every derogatory epithet in the
book of hate because of his alleged pro-Afrikaner sympathies.

Williams met Stead through Stead's friend and correspondent,
Olive Schreiner, the white South African novelist, who wrote of
herself in an undated letter to Stead as one "to whom all broken
or oppressed things, be they prostitutes or South African natives,
are dear to me as though they had sprung from my body." [38] It is
Stead who later told of making Williams's acquaintance while in
Cape Town and who disclosed that it was in Williams's chambers that
"the idea of a federation or league of all the colored races of South
Africa was first mooted," [39] that the decision to form it was taken
at the home of Abdurahman, and that Williams was elected its
president. Williams was evidently a unifying force among the non-
Europeans, and it may be presumed that his associates on the
school board were also involved in the promotion of this federation,
which seemed to be the follow-up to the grand March protest meeting.

According to Stead, the federation included "all natives, Kaffirs,
West Indians, Malays, and Chinamen, although the last-named have no
regular association as yet." Stead did not mention Indians, but because of Gool's membership on the school board and his constant
association with the group, they were probably included.

The league was not as all-embracing as Stead assumed, for the South
African Moslem Association, headed by Hadjie H. N. Effendi, had
decided not to join the South African Citizens' Defence Committee,
as the group was named. [40] The Moslems had fallen victim to the
"divide and rule" tactics of the whites. Effendi reported to his
Association on a meeting held at Abdurahman's home under Abdurahman's chairmanship, which he had attended with his vice-president,
Abdol Majiet. He said they (Majiet and Effendi) had decided not to
participate in the committee because they believed in the word of
"Doctor Jim" (Dr. Leander Starr Jameson, of Jameson raid fame, then
prime minister of Cape Colony and representative of the Rhodes mining

interests). "Doctor Jim" had written Effendi on September 20, 1903, promising "equal rights to all civilized men" and insulting the Africans by adding, "It is only the aboriginal natives we consider uncivilized." [41]

As outlined by Effendi, the Defence Committee planned to carry on a "steady and persistent" agitation to secure for the colored people equal civil and political rights. It planned to help register every colored person entitled to be an elector and to organize the colored vote in municipal elections. It would also raise funds to fight appeals from the lower courts in cases of injustice to colored people and would monitor legislation to see that colored rights were not infringed.

It would appear that the Defence Committee worked at securing the registration of colored voters as it had planned, difficult as this was, for Abdurahman was to be a candidate for the Cape Town municipal council. The 1902 census showed a considerable increase in the population of Cape Town over 1891. The white population went up by 85.14 percent; the "other" (African and colored) by 32.74 percent, probably driven from the countryside as a result of the war. The number of voters had risen 212.32 percent from 5,485 to 17,131. [42] The numbers of nonwhite and white voters were not given separately though the nonwhite would have been the smaller number because of the voter requirement.

Abdurahman's candidacy for the municipal council represented a break with the past. Hitherto the nonwhites had been just "voting cattle" to the white politicians. "They put their cross on ballot papers but never took part in the selection of candidates or in the making of policies." [43] The new strategy was for him to be elected by a show of black voter solidarity. Williams seemed to have taken a leading part in Abdurahman's election campaign. Thus, at a meeting held shortly after nomination day in No. 6 district, a colored stronghold, "on the motion of Advocate Williams, seconded by Dr. Forsyth, a vote of confidence [in the candidate] was unanimously passed." [44]

The appearance for the first time of a colored candidate at a municipal election in South Africa gave it a special significance. African and colored organizations throughout the four colonies took an interest in it and were not disappointed at the results. Out of twelve candidates Abdurahman finished in second place, becoming the first nonwhite councillor in the history of Cape Town, the start of a long political career. He polled 2,307 votes, just 275 fewer than the leader. Predictably, white South African supremacists saw his election as an unsavory development, while Williams and his co-workers were greatly encouraged by it.

In his practice at the bar Williams appeared in a number of routine divorce cases between black parties in the Supreme Court, but there was one other case of special interest in which he figured in the magistrate's court in Tulbagh. It probably added to his reputation among the whites as "a very prominent agent of the Ethiopian Society." It was a case involving the paltry sum of two pounds five shillings arrears of rent and two pounds ten shillings for breach of the "laws" of the Saron Mission of the Rhenish Missionary Society. [45] The society was of German origin with long established missionary centers in South Africa for the colored people. On stations like Saron colored people lived under missionary supervision and were required to conform with rules laid down by the society or its agent. Williams, under instructions from a white attorney, W. Gordon Coulton, appeared as advocate for Sampson Afrika, a member of the Saron Mission who had been sued by the society's agent, Rev. Frederick Eich, for breach of the regulation that "no one may, without the permission of the society, open a shop, bakery or butchery." Afrika, a butcher, had been given notice to leave the station. Williams's defense was that his client was not party to the agreement because it was signed with the "X" mark of an illiterate, whereas his client was literate and always signed his name. Further, his client had "tendered" the rent, which had been refused; and in addition his client denied liability, claiming the "law" about shops, bakeries, and butcheries was unreasonable and so not binding on him.

Afrika's butcher shop in fact was a challenge to European control on the station; it was in competition with a European shop, which he undersold by one penny per pound. Afrika insisted that he had committed no breach; his house was valued at eighty pounds, and, he told the magistrate, he stood to lose it if he was evicted because he would be paid only twenty-two pounds for it under Saron "law." Williams finally told the magistrate that the case was one with far-reaching consequences affecting the status of 2,000 Africans and colored people who for generations past had lived at Saron and who, in many instances, had come into possession of the land from their fathers and grandfathers. They had come to look upon it as their own in perpetuity, so long as they paid the nominal rent required of them. The eviction of his client from the

land that had descended from his grandfather meant that he had to
start anew elsewhere with the wretched compensation offered by the
society. Williams contended that the society had not proved the alleged
signature of Afrika to the "laws"; he had established tender and refusal
of rent, and, assuming that the "laws" were valid, no breach had been
proved to entitle the society to the relief claimed in the summons. When
the magistrate gave judgment in favor of the society with costs, Williams
immediately announced he would appeal. [46]

Some difficulty seems to have arisen in connection with the appeal,
however. The magistrate's clerk claimed that the requirements of the
law had not been complied with and the leave of the court of appeal
had to be obtained to enable it to be heard. Leave was readily given
because of the importance of the case by Chief Justice de Villiers and
Mr. Justice Hopley on the application of Advocate Greer for Afrika. [47]
Williams's absence is not explained but it is possible that Attorney
Coulton felt the case so important that it required a more experienced,
and perhaps influential, counsel because advocate opposing the application was the former Cape attorney-general and prime minister, W. P.
Schreiner.

Williams had rightly judged the vital importance of the case although
only a small sum of money was involved. Afrika finally lost the appeal
but the result led to much protest by the residents not only of Saron
but also of Elim station, who challenged the claim of the Rhenish
Missionary Society to ownership of the land since the grant in 1882 by
the crown had been for missionary purposes only. They opposed the
unilateral introduction of new mission "laws," saying, in a petition to
the attorney-general, that under them "we do not know whether we are
British subjects, Freemen or Slaves or whether we are bound by the
laws of the land." [48]

It was possibly about the time of the Supreme Court application in
Afrika's case that Williams left Cape Town for Basutoland to be the
guest of Chief Lerothodi in his capital for two weeks, and soon afterward he returned to England. Lerothodi may have been the chief who is
said to have told Williams that he was not an African as he spoke no
language of his own, that he was European because he dressed, thought,
and spoke like one. [49] Three years afterward Williams wrote about his
visit to Chief Lerothodi, saying that in those parts of Africa where no

vestige of western civilization had entered, he had enjoyed "the best hospitality and kindness from the people."[50]

Williams appears to have been of two minds about his return to England. There was the call of his family in London where he might be able to get into Parliament to speak for the Africans of the world; on the other hand there was much work to be done in South Africa where his people were hard pressed and his practice was growing in the face of heavy odds.[51]

NOTES

1. In South Africa the term "colored" has been used to refer to people descended from various combinations of indigenous African, Malay, and European stocks.

2. Interview with Mrs. Rogers, daughter of R. W. Wooding, August 25, 1970, in New York City.

3. *Mirror,* July 8, 1901.

4. Williams to Mrs. Williams, November 17, 1903, Williams Papers, Barataria, Trinidad.

5. *Mirror,* March 29, 1911.

6. *Review of Reviews* (March 1905): 250.

7. M. K. Gandhi, *Autobiography: Story of My Experiments with Truth* (Washington, D.C.: Public Affairs Press, 1954), pp. 146, 147.

8. Eric A. Walker, *Lord de Villiers and His Times* (London: Constable, 1925), pp. 112, 113.

9. Certificate of admission, October 29, 1903, Williams Papers.

10. *South Africa,* June 24, 1905.

11. A. J. Garvey, ed., *Philosophy and Opinions of Marcus Garvey* (New York: Atheneum Press, 1969), 1: 61.

12. M. M. Mokone et al., "Synopsis of the Early History of the A. M. E. Church in South Africa," in Bishop L. J. Coppin, *Observations of Persons and Things in South Africa, 1900-1904* (Philadelphia: AME Book Concern, n.d.).

13. *Christian Express,* December 1, 1904.

14. *South African Native Affairs Commission, 1903-05* (London: Darling, 1905), 3: 909.

15. Ibid.

16. Maurice S. Evans, *Black and White in South East Africa* (London: Longmans, 1916), pp. 154, 155.

17. *Cape Argus Weekly,* February 17, 1901.

18. Alexander Walters, *My Life and Work* (New York: Fleming H. Revell Company, 1917), p. 102.

19. D. D. T. Jabavu, *Life of John Tengo Jabavu* (Lovedale, South Africa: Lovedale Institution Press, 1922).

20. *Cape Argus Weekly,* December 30, 1903.

21. Williams to Mrs. Williams, November 17, 1903, Williams Papers.

22. *Cape Argus Weekly,* December 16, 1903.

23. Ibid., December 30, 1903.

24. *Review of Reviews* (March 1905): 250.

25. *South African Review,* March 4, 1904.

26. Ms Brit. Emp. S18. C/91, Anti-Slavery Papers, Rhodes House Library, Oxford. Williams apparently sent a copy of the prospectus to the society. There is an "X" against his name, and below, in his handwriting, "Church Street, Capetown, S.A."

27. Lionel Forman, Chapters in the History of South Africa's March to Freedom, pamphlet, Reel 11, *Miscellaneous South African Documents,* Hoover Institution, Stanford, California.

28. J. S. Marais, *The Cape Coloured People, 1652-1937* (London: Longmans, 1939), p. 159.

29. *Cape Argus Weekly,* February 10, 1904.

30. Printed circular dated September 16, 1902, Tobin Papers, Miscellaneous South African Documents.

31. Flyer, "Mass Meeting of Coloured People on 22 March," Tobin Papers.

32. Poster, "Grievances of the Colored People Residing in the Transvaal," Tobin Papers.

33. Flyer, Tobin Papers.

34. See Richard van der Ross, "The Founding of the African Peoples Organization in Cape Town in 1903 and the Role of Dr. Abdurahman," *Munger Africana Library Notes* 5, 1974-1975.

35. *Cape Times Weekly,* March 30, 1903; see also clipping from the *Owl,* n.d., Tobin Papers.

36. *Review of Reviews* (March 1905): 250.

37. *Cape Times Weekly,* March 30, 1901.

38. S. C. Cronwright-Schreiner, ed., *Letters of Olive Schreiner, 1876-1920* (London: Unwin, 1924), p. 205. Olive Schreiner was the sister of W. P. Schreiner, Cape prime minister and attorney-general.

39. *Review of Reviews* (March 1905): 250.

40. *Cape Times Weekly,* July 20, 1904.

41. Quoted in H. J. Simons and R. E. Simons, *Colour and Class in South Africa, 1850-1950* (Harmondsworth: Penquin, 1969).

42. *South Africa,* July 23, 1904.

43. Simons and Simons, *Colour and Class,* p. 123.

44. *Cape Argus,* September 8, 1904.

45. J. Duplessis, *A History of Christian Missions in South Africa* (London: Longmans, 1911), pp. 200, 240.

46. *Cape Argus,* November 2, 1904.

47. *Cape Times Weekly,* November 29, 1904.

48. *South African Review,* April 7, 1905.

49. Conversations with Mr. H. F. Sylvester Williams in Trinidad, November 1968.

50. *The Jamaican,* September 28, 1907.

51. *Review of Reviews* (March 1905): 250.

Work for Africa in London, 1905-1907

9

Williams was conscious of his blackness but in England it did not weigh heavily on him. He would have been derided by some today as Afro-Saxon, but he believed that the British Constitution knew no color and that with education it was possible for anyone to rise. He believed this extended throughout the British empire and that, wherever the British flag flew, everyone should enjoy the rights of franchise and self-government, trial by a jury of one's peers, and freedom of expression.

He was back in London early in 1905 still with the idea of the early days of the African Association that there should be an African spokesman in Parliament, and, moreover, that he should be that spokesman. His color did not matter; in fact to him it was the very reason why he should be there, and he asserted this with the self-confidence that marked all his actions and utterances. The fact that the Indian Naoroji had been a Liberal member for Deptford seemed to spur him; it was only fair that the Africans in the empire should be represented too, he said. Indeed, justice required it, for the destinies of blacks in the British empire were decided in the House of Commons, and they needed a spokesman.

Soon after his return to England he began looking for a seat in a Liberal constituency to fight the imminent general election and had appeared before a number of constituency selection committees. His reception had been cordial; there had been no objection on the ground of color but he had been too late for this election.[1]

Williams did not let his noncandidacy stop him as a spokesman, though he did this, as he said, "quite informally," at the request of his fellow countrymen who desired him to present their "many and varied" grievances before the government and the public. About this time, for instance, Jabavu in King William's Town wrote to Tobin in Cape Town, saying, "Mr. Sylvester Williams who is now in England can do much to help us there by submitting our requirements to the Secretary of State." [2] Williams had already called at the Colonial Office to present to officials there his views and those of the Africans and coloreds on the constitutions still in preparation for the new colonies of Transvaal and Orange River.

Thus Williams continued to identify himself completely with the black and colored South Africans, whom he referred to as "my people." In relating to Stead the case he had put to the Colonial Office on their behalf, he said he told them that "we" should not be deprived of equal justice because of the color of "our skins." He had asked also for a clause to be entrenched protecting "our civil and political rights" against encroachment by the white colonial legislators. This, of course, was not done but the experience elsewhere since that time, including the liberal Cape Colony, has been that such clauses have proved useless—except where force is used, as in Kenya—where a white minority has been allowed political power in the African colonies and has been persistent in pursuing its goal of depriving the majority blacks of civil and political rights.

Williams put forward other grievances, such as those aired at the March 22 Cape Town meeting and in the proposals of the Citizens' Defence Committee, but he elaborated his views on freedom of religion in the South African context in a manner that, in the South African colonies, would have sustained the suspicion of his being "a very important agent of the Ethiopian Society."[3] Though he was a lifelong member of the Church of England his own spirit of religious toleration was such that he easily grasped the importance of Africans having their own church. Thus he urged at the Colonial Office that the state recognize the African's claim "to institute his own Church, presided over by his own ministers." He thought this would diminish friction because the African trusted "his own man." [4]

If by this time Williams had not arrived at a realistic attitude on the prospects of Britain's keeping its war promises to the South African nonwhites, he at least expressed doubts that the promises could be kept. He feared that unless the practices of Cape Colony were extended to the Zambezi, the Transvaal policy of "exclusion and imposition" would be extended to Table Bay. In this he was prophetic; Britain's promises were flagrantly and cynically broken. The reason given by the Conserva-

tive leader, A. J. Balfour, during a House of Commons debate in May
1908 was, "You cannot . . . give the natives in South Africa equal rights
with the whites without threatening the whole fabric of white civilization."[5] What was at stake was less the fabric of white civilization
than the vast mineral wealth of South Africa. Today the Africans and
colored are under a far greater repression than Williams and his friends
could ever have dreamed.

Williams spoke again unofficially in May 1906 for the chiefs of Cape
Coast, Gold Coast (now Ghana), who sent a delegation to protest against
provisions of a controversial 1894 Town Councils Ordinance now being
applied to the town. Under this law one-half of the council would be
official members, including the district commissioner, who would be
president; the other half would be unofficial members, elected or
nominated by the government.[6] It was a law that had been foisted on
the chiefs who had been demanding without success the institution
of municipalities composed according to pre-European tradition (i.e.,
the chiefs of the town appointed councillors). When the ordinance was
introduced, the chiefs resisted and the people refused to participate in
its working. They had sent a delegation to England to object to the
derogation from their authority. They said the whole council should be
constituted according to custom. But the imperial power refused to
recognize African custom, replacing it by an undemocratic contrivance.

When Williams spoke for the chiefs, his friend James Keir Hardie, the
chairman of the Labour party, introduced him to Lord Elgin, the Liberal
secretary of state for the colonies. Two other MPs, both Liberals,
accompanied them (J. Cathcart Wilson, Harborough, Leicester, and
R. C. Lehmann, Orkney and Shetlands). Elgin rejected their plea; the
Gold Coast government, he said, was to contribute half the council's
revenue, and because the council was new, it did not seem unreasonable to him that some of the members be nominated.

It was probably in 1906 that Williams became involved in a new
organization, the League of Universal Brotherhood and Native Races
Association, whose motto was "United to Aid" and its symbol a
black hand and a white hand clasped in greeting.[7] Williams was the
only black member of the committee of the organization, in which
the religious element was strongly represented. One of the vice-presidents, the Rev. F. B. Meyer, was the head of the Free Church Council
and had contributed money to the 1900 Pan-African Conference. It

was not an organization on the lines of the Pan-African Association nor even of the African Association; its aims must be guessed from its name.

One of the few things we know about it is that Williams enlisted its aid in 1907 in fighting the case for two branches of the Basuto nation deprived of their lands in Orange River Colony. It may have been as a result of Williams's visit in 1904 to Lerothodi, king of the Basutos, that the case of the displaced Basutos was entrusted to him. In January 1970, a party consisting of three chiefs, Lesisa, Moloi, and Lequila, with Joseph Gumede, their interpreter and counselor, and two attendants, arrived in London. They represented the Batlokoa and Babhukukwe tribes, which comprised some 25,000 persons scattered over Orange River Colony, Natal, and Zululand. They had been dispossessed of their lands by the emigrant Boers in their northward flight from British rule. Later the Boers had granted them land in the Harrismith district in return for military service and the payment of seven thousand head of cattle to the representative of the Free State government. The Africans had occupied the land from 1869 to 1882 when they were forcibly ejected by the Orange Free State authorities because they had helped the British in the Zulu war of 1879 and in the Boer war of 1880-1881. The tribe scattered. In the recent South African war they had been enlisted by the British as scouts and in return for this service had received certificates acknowledging their assistance from the British authorities. The British had also taken and used their cattle and horses, promising to pay after the war, but they had not been compensated.

After the British victory, the Orange Free State had become Orange River Colony, so the Africans petitioned the lieutenant-governor for the return of their land or compensation for it. They also asked for the repeal of the Free State law of 1893 (no more than five Africans could live on one farm) which the British reenacted. Their plea failed. They were told that communal tenure was not allowed, that the land was already occupied, and that they could not be allowed to settle as a tribe in the neighborhood. The government offered to settle them on farms owned by white farmers where they could have a little patch to cultivate for themselves and receive wages for labor on the farms. The Africans had refused, and when they asked to buy the land they were turned down. Their next step was to go to London to ask King

Edward VII, whom they regarded as their king and paramount chief, to allow them a location where they might live as free men together or make it constitutional for them to buy land in their own names. The Basutos' plight attracted wide attention, and Reuters News Agency circulated an interview with Williams stating their case.[8] The week before the Basuto delegation called on Lord Elgin, Williams delivered a memorandum on their case to the Colonial Office.

Williams probably hoped that his mission would be at least as "successful" as one from South Africa in November of the previous year, which had resulted in Lord Elgin's disallowing a Transvaal law denying Indians the right to buy land. That delegation had consisted of Mohandas K. Gandhi and H. O. Ali, representing the Transvaal British Indian Committee. Probably through the intervention of Dadabhai Naoroji, who, as a former Liberal MP, was able to obtain the support of former colleagues, Gandhi and Ali were able to address a large number of Liberal MPs and to enlist some of the most influential of them to join their delegation to Elgin.

The law was disallowed but in fact the disallowance was soon to prove of no value because of the previous grant of self-government to the Transvaal. In vetoing the law, Elgin had merely stalled for time. The new constitution for the Transvaal was promulgated on December 6 shortly after the Gandhi-Ali mission left England to return to South Africa. Under it the franchise was to be extended to whites only, and so the representations that Williams had made on behalf of blacks in South Africa had been in vain. On March 21, 1907, within a month of its election under the lilywhite franchise, Louis Botha's Het Volk party reintroduced the objectionable anti-Indian law, getting it passed by unanimous vote of both houses at a single sitting.[9] Elgin, when appealed to, refused to intervene. A self-governing state, he cynically said, had "the right to go to the devil in its own way." [10]

When he went to the Colonial Office for the Basuto delegation, Williams was accompanied by two Liberal MPs, E. H. Pickersgill and F. W. Wilson, and four members of the League of Universal Brotherhood and Native Races Association. During his ninety-minute interview with Elgin, Williams, who introduced the delegation, explained at length the grievances of the tribes and pleaded for redress.

It took about five weeks for Elgin's reply to reach the Rev. Dr. Charles Garnett, the secretary of the League of Universal Brother-

hood.[11] The high commissioner in South Africa hàd to be consulted
and Lord Selborne advised that the Orange River Colony government
had investigated and decided that there was not sufficient justification
to interfere with the rights of the white occupants of the area in
question. Elgin himself had stated that while he would view with satisfaction the passing of legislation that would enable the natives to
buy land in their own names, as they could in the Transvaal, he felt
that he must leave the matter to the new elective legislature. Again
Elgin was being cynical, for there was little hope of the Basutos'
getting justice from a legislature elected by whites only. In fact, he
left them at the mercy of the white settlers. Further, by advising them
to consider carefully the local government's offer to place them among
the white farming community, he was telling them to submit to slavery.

Elgin's unsatisfactory reply was received in time to be read at the
annual meeting of the League of Universal Brotherhood on March 27,
with Dr. Evans Darby, one of the vice-presidents, in the chair. After
Dr. Garnett had read Elgin's letter, Williams moved a resolution, which
was passed, expressing the hope that Elgin would soon be in a position
to advise the king to make a satisfactory reply to the chiefs' petition. Keir
Hardie then moved a resolution protesting the policy being pursued toward the Africans of Natal and urging the imperial government to direct
that the ministers of the colony deal with them more sympathetically and
thus prevent a recurrence of hostilities. This was a reference to the
massacre in early 1906 of the followers of the chief Bambata in their
opposition to the poll tax. [12] Keir Hardie hoped the Basuto chiefs
would continue their agitation at home in a legitimate way, and he
recommended that a small commission of enquiry should be appointed
to investigate the whole question.

Between the deputation to Elgin and receipt of his reply to the
Basutos' plea, Williams and Gumede witnessed the opening of Parliament by the king from seats in the royal gallery of the House of
Lords. Their tickets were provided "with the Lord Great Chamberlain's Compliments," and Williams kept his own as a souvenir, noting
on it: "Two tickets for the Royal Gallery To view the Opening of Parl:
on 12th Feb. 07—Mr. Gumede and I attend. The Procession was
grand—The King and Queen noticed us repeatedly."[13] Because of
the invitations to the royal gallery and because the king noticed their
presence, it can be assumed that King Edward had previously received

the Basuto chiefs with Williams and Gumede and recognized them
among the guests viewing the ceremony.

The Basuto chiefs sailed for home ten days after the meeting.
Williams must have been gravely disappointed with the results of
his efforts and despaired of any improvement in the lot of the people
whom he had left behind in South Africa. The Colored African Political Organization had sent its president, Williams's friend, Abdurahman,
to London in July 1906 seeking amendment of the Transvaal and
Orange River constitutions that would grant voting rights to the colored people. But he had had no greater success than Williams had in
his fight for the Basutos. Abdurahman returned home a disappointed
man. [14]

Meanwhile Williams carried on his practice of the law, which he
had resumed upon deciding not to return to South Africa. [15] The
"severe boycott" he had been subjected to by the majority of his
fellow members of the Cape bar probably made him decide not to
return to South Africa. [16] He had reported to Stead, who thought him
"a man of extraordinary pluck," that he had sought the intervention
of the benchers of Gray's Inn in the matter but obviously to no avail.

By this time Williams had become involved in municipal politics
as a member of the Marylebone Borough Council. In order to further
his political career he had secured membership in the prestigious National Liberal Club. [17] He had probably decided that if he wanted to
be elected to Parliament and to be official spokesman for blacks in
the British empire, he would have to serve an apprenticeship. Thus
he took on the role of a Progressive candidate for a seat on the
borough council of Marylebone, which was situated in his home
suburb of St. John's Wood.

His scope in the borough council was restricted to local matters
without the remotest connection with national or imperial affairs,
but being a councillor could keep him in the limelight as a potential
parliamentary candidate. It was a brave hope, but a precedent had been
set by Naoroji the Indian, who had been elected to Parliament from
Deptford to represent English constituents and to fight the cause of
India. In like manner Williams expected to be elected by English people,
for the black electorate in London was tiny.

Encouraged by Councillor E. Connelly, an Irish fellow member of
Ward 3 West Marylebone Liberal and Radical Association, Williams

offered himself and was chosen by the ward committee as one of
three Progressive and six Progressive and Labour candidates to con-
test the nine seats for the No. 3 (Church) Ward, not far from his home.

Marylebone was a Conservative stronghold. The Conservatives' Liberal opponents, the Progressives, were in alliance with Labour candidates,
representing the trade unions, the new socialist movement, and the
Labour party, whose demands for social justice were just beginning to
have an impact on the consciences of the holders of power. The work-
ing-class members of the Liberal and Radical Association who had the
support of their trade unions used the label "Progressive and Labor."

Williams's links with the trade union members among his colleagues
seem to have been closer than with his fellow Progressive candidates
of Ward 3. He had the backing of the Workers' Union, whose general
secretary, Charles Duncan, MP, gave him sound advice and support.
The union was one of the kind conceived by its vice-president, the militant Tom Mann, as a "union of all workers—a new 'political-cum-trades
union party,' . . . an amalgamated confederation of all kinds—brain workers and manual workers."[18] In the 1890s Mann, who was to become a
legendary figure in the trade union movement, had been a member of
the Afro-American Ida Wells's Anti-Lynching Committee in England. [19]

Williams was the only Progressive candidate in his ward who
appeared with his Progressive and Labour colleagues at Sunday morning street-corner meetings. He declared plainly that if he was elected
he would serve the working classes. It must have been strange to some
of his hearers that a black man was seeking to be their representative
though he was a professional man. Others may have taken pride in him
as a product of their empire. Williams probably encountered race prejudice in knocking on the doors of ratepayers, canvassing their votes.

Williams won a seat, becoming probably the first black man to be
elected to public office in Britain, but the election was a disaster for
the Progressives in Marylebone and especially in Ward 3, the "Fighting Ward." The Conservatives (Municipal Reformers) won five of
nine seats in Ward 3, Progressives three, and a Progressive running
as an independent was also returned. Williams was in eighth place with
701 votes. Yet Ward 3 represented the Progressives' best effort in
Marylebone for they won only two seats in the other eight wards.

The Progressives suffered reverses in other elections in towns throughout the country, to the delight of the Conservative press. The *Pall Mall Gazette,* for instance, spoke of the "sustained sharp reverses" of "Mr. Keir Hardie's party" (Labour), whose policy it equated with "an arrogant and ambitious communism" while calling that of the Progressives "socialistic."[20]

To acquaint the ratepayers with the backgrounds of their new representatives, the *Mercury* published short biographies. Williams's showed a record of achievement as considerable as that of any and greater than that of many of his colleagues. Apart from mention of his having convened "the first Pan-African Conference ever held in London," there was not an inkling that he might be other than a white Englishman. He had been an advocate of the Supreme Court of Cape Colony, had visited the king of the Basutos, and had represented "the natives of South Africa and those of the Gold Coast of West Africa at the Colonial Office"—all consistent with the conduct of a well-meaning, humanitarian Englishman trying to help downtrodden blacks. An unwitting English reader could conclude that Councillor Henry Sylvester Williams (Progressive) was upper middle class and a member of the establishment though he was born in Trinidad. He had a university education—Dalhousie and King's College—was a member of one of the learned professions, belonged to the exclusive National Liberal Club in the West End and the International Law Association, and was a Fellow of the Royal Society of Arts. He had traveled through Canada and the United States and visited South Africa, had one publication to his credit, was the son-in-law of a major in the Royal Marines, had a St. John's Wood address and chambers in the Temple.[21]

Williams settled down to the work of municipal councillor. He was selected to serve on two standing committees—legal and parliamentary, and improvements and housing—which passed on their recommendations for approval at the fortnightly meetings of the whole council. Because the opposition (his side) was small, he had greater scope for activity. Williams figured as an advocate of economy, criticizing the majority for saying there was no money when called upon to provide a path over a railroad for the safety of his constituents while asking later for an increase in the borough surveyor's salary.

Williams took an active part in the council's ceremonial program. For example, he attended the mayor's garden party, accompanied by his wife, and the mayor's banquet, and took part in Citizen Sunday when the new mayor, accompanied by the aldermen and councilors and the town clerk, went in state to a service in the Church of England parish church.

Service as a councillor was not to deflect Williams from his interest in and devotion to Africa. News of his election was to bring about the renewal of contact with an elderly Canadian friend, whom he apparently had met during his stay in Canada Sir Henri Gustave Joly de Lotbinière had been one of the fathers of confederation, a Protestant premier of Roman Catholic Quebec, a minister in the dominion government, and finally lieutenant-governor of British Columbia.[22] Not having heard from Williams for years, he had made enquiries about him of friends in the West Indies, one of whom sent him a newspaper clipping reporting his election.

Williams had made a great impression on Sir Henri who wrote, "I could not forget you, and something told me that I would hear of you doing good work."[23] He was curious to know from "dear Mr. Williams." as he addressed him, "who are those who voted to elect you" and how, as a black man, he was getting on at the bar. [24] Williams's letters in reply to his friend have not been found; they might have revealed some of his innermost thoughts on race for he apparently confided in Sir Henri, who discussed the question with him. Williams had sent him an invitation to the annual meeting of the League of Universal Brotherhood and a clipping from *John Bull Over-Seas* referring to him and his fight for the Basutos. He replied, encouraging Williams in the "great work" before him, advising that he should go "simply and patiently on your way, conscious of your manhood" so that his example would speak louder than words.[25]

NOTES

1. *Review of Reviews* (March 1905): 250.

2. Jabavu to Tobin, February 4, 1905, Tobin Papers, Miscellaneous South African Documents, Hoover Institution, Stanford, California.

3. Wallis to Grey, February 25, 1908, F. P. 367/85, Public Record Office, London.

4. *Review of Reviews* (March 1905): 251.

5. A. P. Thórnton, *The Imperial Idea and Its Enemies* (New York: St. Martins Press, 1959), p. 159.

6. *Times,* May 5, 1906. See also Francis Agbodeka, *African Politics and British Policy in the Gold Coast, 1868-1900* (Evanston: Northwestern University Press, 1971), pp. 128-129.

7. Leaflet, Williams Papers, Barataria, Trinidad.

8. *South Africa,* January 12, 1907.

9. H. J. Simons and R. E. Simons, *Class and Colour In South Africa, 1850-1890* (Harmondsworth: Penguin, 1969), p. 71.

10. Edward Roux, *Time Longer Than Rope* (Madison: University of Wisconsin Press, 1964).

11. Dr. Garnett was chairman of Marcus Garvey's first public meeting in London at Royal Albert Hall, London, June 6, 1928. A. J. Garvey, *Garvey and Garveyism* (Kingston, Jamaica, 1963), p. 182.

12. See Shula Marks, *Reluctant Rebellion* (Oxford: Clarendon Press, 1970).

13. Ticket with note thereon, Williams Papers.

14. *South Africa,* August 25, 1906.

15. Ibid., January 12. 1907.

16. *Review of Reviews* (March 1905): 250.

17. Goss Billson, secretary, National Liberal Club, to the author, July 13, 1970.

18. *New Age,* February 10, 1898.

19. Ida Wells (Ida Wells-Barnett), *Red Record* (Chicago: Donohue and Henneberry, 1894), p. 78.

20. *Pall Mall Gazette,* November 2, 1906.

21. *Marylebone Mercury and West London Gazette,* November 17, 1906.

22. William S. Wallace, *Dictionary of Canadian Biography* (Toronto: Macmillan, 1945).

23. De Lotbinière to Williams, December 6, 1906, Williams Papers.

24. Ibid., May 8, 1907, Williams Papers.

25. Ibid., April 6, 1907, and fragment marked "page 3," n.d., Williams Papers.

Protecting Liberian Interests **10**

President Arthur Barclay of Liberia arrived in London on August 29, 1907, on an official mission to England and France to discuss frontier and other problems with the two governments that had colonies adjoining the Liberian republic, whose territory had been seriously reduced by their encroachments. He was also seeking a loan of a half-million dollars to finance development. In the president's party were Frederick E. R. Johnson, secretary of state, and Thomas McCants Stewart, who was deputy attorney-general of the Liberian Boundary Commission. Johnson had taken a prominent part in the Pan-African Conference in 1900. Stewart, who had once advocated the settlement of "only our best people physically and mentally"[1] in Liberia, was now on his third trip there. During a brief first stay in 1883 and 1884 he had been on the faculty of Liberia College. Since his recent return, after seventeen years in law and politics in New York and Hawaii, Stewart had begun to codify the republic's laws and was concerned with solving the pressing boundary problems. [2]

President Barclay's official movements in London, reported in *The Times,* included visits to the Foreign Office and the Colonial Office and an audience with King Edward VII at Buckingham Palace. His visit to Paris to confer with President Fallières and the minister of foreign affairs resulted in an agreement with France ending the long-standing Franco-Liberian border dispute before his return to London.

Williams was happy to meet Johnson once again. He recalled Stewart's activities as a lawyer and political figure in New York, but he was especially impressed with President Barclay, whom he interviewed for the *Jamaican* before the president's visit to Paris. He wrote: "All [Johnson, Stewart, and Barclay] are truly representative of the African Race, and in whom we may be proud." He noted that

Barclay, a Barbadian by birth, had retained his Barbadian accent although he had left Barbados when he was only eleven years old. According to Williams, Barclay was "prepossessing in appearance and strikingly handsome." [3]

Williams was well briefed on Liberian affairs. He wrote that the object of Barclay's visit was to settle "once and for all every and any discrepancy which may have arisen, and calculated to disturb the tranquility of the Republic by the undue influence of Resident Consuls." [4] This was a pointed reference to Captain Charles Braithwaite Wallis, the British consul in Monrovia, who was in London and, according to protocol, in attendance at President Barclay's meetings with British officials. Wallis had the greatest contempt for Liberians, and his interference in the country's affairs was to be highlighted by the February 1909 incident, which Liberians believed was "part of a plot" by British subjects in Liberia to make it appear that the government was falling and to bring about a British occupation. [5]

From his conversations with Barclay, Williams formed a most favorable impression about Liberia and its people. He found "this great man" totally devoid of self-aggrandizement. He was impressed by the fact that when Africa was largely and rapidly coming under European colonial rule, the idea uppermost in Barclay's mind was the "retention of the Lone Star as a heritage for future African generations." He also found Barclay very alive to "the criticisms and objections to the few Black states." [6] One result of Williams's meeting with the party was an invitation to visit Liberia the following January for the jubilee of the founding of Liberia and to address the second annual meeting of the Liberian National Bar Association, of which Johnson was president-elect and Stewart secretary.

Williams left for Liberia immediately after attending the first meeting for the year of the Marylebone Borough Council held on January 18, 1908. Soon after he arrived in Monrovia, Williams entered into a deed of lease of land—three hundred acres—at Brewerville Settlement in Montserrado County, near the Poah River. The parties were described as "Elijah Lincoln Parker, farmer, of the settlement of Brewerville, in the County of Montserrado . . . and Henry Sylvester Williams, gentleman, of 50 Hamilton Gardens, St. John's Wood, London, England." The lease was to be for a term of fifteen years beginning June 1, 1908, with option for renewal on the same terms. The rent was to be

$700 per annum "payable on the legal days of June in each and every year during the continuance of the lease."[7] Williams must have balked at taking citizenship, which is a prerequisite to holding real property in Liberia,[8] because of his wife's position: she could not be admitted to citizenship because of the constitutional bar limiting citizenship to "persons of color."[9]

Williams and his hosts would have been shocked had they realized that his visit was of such concern to the British consul that it was to be the subject of three denunciatory confidential dispatches in two weeks.[10] Whatever Consul Wallis's outward conduct may have been, he had no respect or sympathy for Liberia, its institutions, or its people. To him the Liberian National Bar Association, formed two years previously to improve the standing of the lawyer's profession, was "as big a farce and as great a fraud as the rest of Liberian institutions."[11] He appeared to believe that Liberia was a British protectorate now that President Barclay's visit to London had resulted in a loan from Britain and the president had pledged, on British urgings, to institute certain reforms.

The loan was obtained for the republic by the Liberian Development Company headed by Sir Harry Johnston in return for a concession to exploit the country's resources and on the understanding that $25,000 was to be allocated to meet the country's pressing debts, $35,000 for operating expenses of the company, $125,000 for payment of internal debts, and $315,000 for unspecified "banking and road" projects. The loan was secured against the republic's customs revenue, involving a derogation of the country's sovereignty by placing the company's representatives in full control of the Liberian Customs Service.[12] Johnston, a former British consul in West and Central Africa who had been responsible for the removal and exile of King Jaja of Opobo, had the approval and support of the British Foreign Office in the formation of the company as well as in securing the participation of French capital. The idea of French participation was to involve France so that the two rival countries, by controlling Liberia politically through the company and sharing the spoils of exploitation, could avoid open conflict. The project was a failure: the Liberian government and Johnston quarreled, the company's charter was revoked, and the Liberian government assumed direct responsibility for the loan.

The reform measures the British government had impressed
on President Barclay were the strengthening of the customs administration by the appointment of three additional British
officials; the establishment of an adequate frontier force under
European officers; and the reform of the treasury and the reform
of the judiciary. After Barclay's return to Liberia, according to
the United States Senate report, "Affairs in Liberia,"[13] these
suggestions were presented to Liberia in a letter from Wallis "in
rather more peremptory terms." Wallis said that if the reforms
were carried out within six months, Great Britain would be dis-
posed to help, but, if not, it would "be inclined to demand immediate adjustment of all pending questions."

The Liberian government, the report stated, endeavored to the
best of its ability to do what was expected of it. It appointed new
customs officials, passed a law creating a frontier force under European
officers, and took steps to establish the chief inspector of customs as
the financial adviser of the republic. To comply with the terms agreed
upon with the French, two thousand square miles of hinterland were
ceded to France.

In an atmosphere in which British interests were being unduly pressed
on the Liberian government, the presence of an American black among
them warning them to be on guard against foreign encroachments was
enough to excite dismay. Consul Wallis feared that Deputy Attorney-General Stewart might turn the scale in favor of the United States. Because
Williams "appears to be a friend" of Stewart's, Consul Wallis deemed
him guilty by association. He wrote on February 11 that "for that reason,
I am rather suspicious of him." Stewart was "an absolute humbug . . . and
a danger to British and Liberian interests."[14]

In his first dispatch dated February 16 and devoted wholly to
Williams and Stewart, Wallis said that Williams seemed to have "mixed
himself up a good deal" in politics, and it was rumored that he was
connected with "this proposed American Mission."

A short dispatch two days later was devoted solely to Williams.
Wallis had "since learnt that this gentleman was turned out of South
Africa during the war for disloyalty and for preaching seditious doctrines to the natives against the white man." He wanted to be "absolutely just to Mr. Williams" and therefore mentioned that he had no proof
of his statements although he believed his source of information was relia-
ble. [15]

If Stewart did not enjoy the confidence of the British consul, he was held in high esteem by his fellow Liberians and their government, to whose well-being he devoted his talents. He advised that Liberia should cultivate the friendship of the United States, which, he said, might prove useful if Liberia needed arbitration, though in approaching the United States they must be "wise as serpents and harmless as doves."[16]

It was in this disturbed atmosphere that Williams made his visit. His appearance before the National Bar Association was a grand occasion. He had in his audience not only the president of the republic but also members of the cabinet, senators, representatives, and the judges of the Supreme Court, and the venue was the executive mansion, home of the president. The topic of his address was "The Object of a Bar Association," and what he said directly on it was of only passing interest.[17] Instead he focused on the dangers by which the country was beset and warned the audience to be on guard.

He noted that Liberia had been encountering adversity; it was attacked by international travelers and writers, as well as by governments with large spheres of influence that would not be satisfied to develop only the vast territories they already controlled. For that reason it was extremely important that every Liberian and every sympathizer of Liberia be very careful and judicious for fear they might find themselves submitting to "insidious usurpation."

Williams pointed out that since Liberia had been recognized by Britain in 1848, all the other African states on the same coast had been taken over by European governments. Their subjects were being made to "swallow the dirt of scorn, contempt and even slavery" at the hands of the "pretentious invader." He cited as an example King Jaja's deportation from Opobo in 1886 by Vice-Consul Harry Johnston, who, he pointed out, was the same person who was the promoter of the Liberian Development Company. He added that King Jaja's people had now "erected a monument in the form of a bronze statue to his memory." Then he turned to poetry to express the "Africa for the Africans" theme, later espoused by Marcus Garvey and denounced by Du Bois after his 1921 Pan-African Congress in Paris.[18] Williams declared:

Breathes there a man with soul so dead
Who has not said this is my land, my native land,
Surely, Africa's the African's.[19]

He warned that Liberia, the symbol of the African's ability to govern, would be pounced upon and "quartered" by the European powers "for the merest international sin." Those powers were "predisposed to stop at nothing" to accomplish their most anxious wish—to "wrest the control and government of Liberia from the hands of Africans." For him it was a sign of European contempt for Liberia that the black republic had not been invited to attend the Hague Peace Conference of 1907 which was attended by forty-eight sovereign states gathered to seek ways to peacefully settle international disputes and lessen the horrors of war.

This address showed Williams was well above the level of a mere municipal councillor; he was capable of thought on the higher plane of international politics for which the opportunity was lacking to vast numbers of Africans subjected to colonial rule or subordinate status in other lands. "The Love of Liberty Brought Us Here," declares the national motto of Liberia, and Williams reacted to the atmosphere. In 1900 the "Address to the Nations" at the Pan-African Conference had called on the imperialist nations to respect the integrity of Liberia. Now he did not scruple to condemn Britain (though he did not name the country), which was one of the European powers waiting to "pounce upon and quarter" Liberia.

Another address by Williams raised Wallis's anger. The consul obtained a report of it in an affidavit from James Lionel Harris, who may have been sent to the meeting by Wallis. Son of an English father and an American mother, Harris described himself as a "subject" of the United States. To Wallis he was "a young white engineer from London" who had arrived January 10 to work for the Liberian government on the road left unfinished by the Liberian Development Company. Harris had attended a "Liberian meeting," which Williams had addressed in a church. He reported that Williams said that in South Africa the British government treated the Africans like "surfs" [sic], that the Zulu war had been forced upon the Zulus by the British government, and that if an African slept in a town without permission he was sent without trial to work in the mines for five years. He quoted Williams as also saying that Liberians should "resist with all their power anything English," that England "wanted" the country, and that he could procure "discontented" West Indians to come to Liberia and help build it.[20]

In Harris's view the address, so far as the British government was concerned, was "treasonable."

Harris's affidavit was appended to Wallis's third dispatch in which the consul affirmed that the suspicions he had formed about Williams were correct. He was convinced that Williams was "a most dangerous character to British interests in Africa and in the Empire's tropical possessions generally, where ever the African is met with."[21]

One major source of Wallis's information was Major R. Mackay Cadell, an English militia officer who had seen service in South Africa and had been selected, through Wallis's instrumentality, to organize the new Liberian frontier force. He had been given a free hand and was subject to only slight supervision by the president himself. Whether by reason of his service in South Africa or otherwise, Cadell was apparently imbued with the white supremacist feelings so predominant among South African whites. It was he who "by chance saw and recognized the man [Williams] here, having come across him during the war in South Africa." [22] (If Cadell came across Williams in South Africa, as he may well have done, it would not have been during the war. Williams had not been called to the bar and did not leave London for South Africa until well after the Treaty of Vereeniging had brought the war to an end.)

According to Cadell's information, Williams was "practically deported" from the Transvaal for endeavoring to incite the natives against the British, and he was "a very prominent agent of the Ethiopian Society." A handwritten marginal notation to Wallis's February 25 dispatch rightly queries, "What is the distinction between practical deportation and deportation?" But Cadell had said more; he charged that because of Williams's "anti-English" leanings, the attorneys of the Transvaal had combined to exclude him from practicing in the courts. He had commenced practice in Johannesburg and then gone to Pretoria, both places "refusing to have anything to do with him." According to the dispatch, Williams was said to have traveled about South Africa spreading the doctrine of "the country for the black races alone" and was believed to have afterward "passed into Swaziland."

There is no confirmation of any such widespread travel by Williams in the capacity of agitator. Yet his alleged exclusion from practice in Johannesburg and Pretoria tends to confirm the story of the boycott

against him in Cape Colony told to Stead on his return from South
Africa. Cadell seems to have followed Williams's movements very
closely; his information might have been derived either from military
intelligence or from officers' mess gossip on what all whites feared
and labeled "Ethiopian" activities. Anyone who "turns a hand" to
help nonwhites in South Africa was suspected of sympathy with the
"so-called Ethiopian Movement," wrote an Afro-American sea captain, Harry Dean, in his story of his adventures in South Africa about
this time. [23] Cadell even had heard about the shooting in Williams's
chambers in Cape Town but distorted it, probably deliberately, in
such a way as to discredit Williams. According to the dispatch,
Williams had thwarted an attempt on his life by a man whom he was
supposed to have "robbed of title deeds, etc."; in the fracas, a client
in his office had been killed. "The man was tried, convicted, but on
the evidence received only a nominal sentence," the dispatch inaccurate-
ly asserted. Cadell's subsequent conduct in Liberia, for which he was ad-
versely criticized by a United States commission, shows that he shared
Wallis's contempt for Liberians. Wallis's account showed that he was
also familiar with Williams's general career in England.

Wallis had learned of Williams's plan to visit Sierra Leone and Guinea
to compare British and French colonial rule. Therefore he had taken
the "precaution" of warning the governor of Sierra Leone that Williams
was a subversive. Wallis was really perturbed; he inquired of the British
foreign secretary, to whom the dispatch was addressed, about steps he
could take against "individuals of this sort, who come here and create
untold mischief." He specifically asked: "Can such individuals as these
when they are British subjects, be arrested, turned out of the country, and
handed over to a British Court for trial?"[24] Here was "a man, a British
subject," he complained, coming into a foreign country straight from
London and opening "a hostile and seditious campaign" against the
British government and the British nation generally. Then he added
that this would be bad enough "in a civilized country" but in Liberia
it was far worse.

Wallis saw himself in the role of a pro-consul manning an embattled
outpost of empire and carrying on the Anglo-Saxon's civilizing mission
against overwhelming odds. He described what he was doing as "trying, amidst great difficulties to reform this Republic" and assist it
to maintain its independence by "dragging it out of a state of chaos."

But, at a critical moment, when he, "surrounded by enemies, and practically cut off from all communication," was doing his utmost to get the reforms accepted, there appeared on the scene "this man Williams" who, with the assistance of McCants Stewart "and the like," was doing his best to ruin "the whole business."

The fact is Williams had not said anything he had not said before or would not have said publicly and with impunity in England. It was true about the mistreatment of blacks in South Africa and it was no crime to advise Liberians to guard their independence. To have advised them to submit to British occupation or connive with the British consul in any plan against Liberia would have been a betrayal of the pan-Africanism he had espoused and fostered. An accusation of sedition or treason was far-fetched, and the question about arresting British subjects in a foreign country did no credit to a British consul. Indeed it was further evidence of Wallis's contempt for Liberian independence. Williams probably never fully realized what a stir his visit to Liberia had made in some British circles.

Wallis's informant, Cadell, described by the United States Commission of Enquiry of the following year as "a man of undoubted energy, but guileless of tact," was later dismissed from the command of the Liberian frontier force after he had written a threatening letter to President Barclay. He had enlisted British subjects from Sierra Leone in the force and had refused to dismiss them. His letter called on the president to pay, within twenty-four hours, money said to be due to the troops or he would not be responsible for the maintenance of order or the president's safety. He sailed for England, followed by his brother officers, leaving the Liberian government to pay "a considerable unauthorized debt."[25]

The sequel to President Barclay's London visit bore out the warnings of Williams and Stewart. The U. S. commission reported that between February 4 and 12, 1909, "intense anti-British feeling" arose among all classes of Liberians. On February 4 the British consul in Monrovia cabled London that the lives of foreign residents were in danger and asked that a gunboat be sent for their protection. On February 10 a British gunboat anchored off Monrovia. It was learned afterward that a British regiment in Sierra Leone was under orders to proceed to Monrovia. Between February 10 and 12 Cadell precipitated his rupture with the government.

The commission, which reported that "foreigners were never for one moment in danger," commented that but for the prompt action of President Barclay the situation would have found a British gunboat in Monrovia harbor, a British officer in command of the frontier force and a large number of British subjects in the ranks, a British official in charge of the Liberian customs, a British officer in command of the Liberian gunboat *Lark*, and a British regiment in the streets of Monrovia.[26] The commission found a widespread belief among Liberians that all this was part of a plot by British subjects in Liberia to make it appear that the Liberian government was tottering to its fall and bring about a British occupation of Monrovia.

The Barclay government, according to Lynch, was satisfied that Blyden, who had been in Liberia during Williams's visit in 1908, had helped in Cadell's attempted coup.[27] Blyden lost his pension from the Liberian government, which apparently felt that his unpatriotic action was the result of his belief that if the country came under British protection, it would be saved from French or German occupation.

The U. S. commission condemned Wallis and Cadell. It found that the reforms Britain pressed on Liberia had "failed of complete realization" because of the "bungling of British officials" and that Wallis had displayed "an utter lack of diplomatic qualifications" for the role of adviser to a foreign power.

Williams had left Monrovia sometime before February 25, the date of Wallis's third dispatch reporting his intention to study French colonial rule in Guinea. His visit afforded him a better appreciation of Liberian realities and the external pressures that the country endured. It would have confirmed his belief that the pioneers needed the help of resolute, self-reliant black men from the New World, and he probably was disappointed that circumstances had made it impossible for him to set the example.

He left for Konakry and if, as Wallis reported, he was going from there to Sierra Leone, it meant his taking ship from Monrovia to Konakry and returning westward to Freetown before heading back to England. He evidently visited both places, for in 1909 he spoke with approval of the French colonial rule in West Africa and compared Freetown unfavorably with Port-of-Spain and San Fernando in Trinidad. He claimed to have been impressed that "the native man" in the French colonies could enjoy the franchise and could be elected to the Conseil Général and eventually sent to represent his people in the Chamber of Deputies in Paris.[28] But his references to the franchise and representation of Africans in the French West African colonies were too sweeping. These liberal provisions applied only to the "four old communes" of Senegal whose inhabitants alone had the status of French citizens (the rest were subjects) and elected a deputy to the French Parliament. The deputies elected in those days were all mulattoes (the first black African being Blaise Diagne, elected in 1914, who presided over Du Bois's Pan-African Congress in Paris in 1919).[29] On the other hand he referred to the British as "somewhat backward in recognizing the ability of black men in the colonies."

There have been suggestions that Williams also visited Nigeria, but there is no evidence to support this. It is said that it was there he became so ill with what might have been blackwater fever that the doctors gave him up; his life was saved by an African woman who administered to him an infusion of geranium roots.[30] His recovery must have been rapid indeed for on March 26 he was present at his first council general meeting since that of January 16. Thereafter he attended most of the fortnightly general meetings, the last being that of August 1. By mid-August he had put his household effects up for sale and was on his way home to Trinidad. Possibly the severe illness in Africa spurred him to seek the perpetual summer of home in place of the chill winds of the coming autumn and the fog, damp, and cold of London's winter.

If he had become disillusioned by conditions in England, there was one thing he must have been sorry to leave—a project for a black students' club in Oxford. He had a letter from John Thomas, a black student at Oxford, inviting his aid in the establishment of a kind of Pan-African students' club.[31] Thomas wanted Williams to send him names and addresses of black students in London. Thomas also asked Williams for the "full name of the young man I met at your house," but made it plain that he wanted "only such names as identify themselves with the race and not those who try to explain themselves away as something else." Among Thomas's race-proud friends in London was Davidson Don Tengo Jabavu, who had been sent to England by his father, Williams's friend, John Tengo Jabavu of Cape Colony. Young Jabavu was then reading for the Bachelor of Arts degree of London University after attending boarding school in Colwyn Bay, North

Wales. He had arrived in England in 1903 following the refusal to admit him to Dale College, King Williams Town, because, according to the school authorities, the "whole question of mixed schools would be introduced" if he were admitted. [32]

But the black Oxford club lost Williams's active support and the students from Africa and the West Indies lost in the Williams's home a warm and friendly meeting place. The ratepayers of Ward 3 lost their councillor and Parliament a possible spokesman for Africa. Charles Duncan's hope that Williams "would stick to the work" was not fulfilled.

Williams seemed to have suddenly abandoned his two major alternatives: to continue to be a black spokesman in England or to settle and work in Liberia. He opted instead to return to his native Trinidad. Of the three alternatives, this was the most unlikely from a Pan-African perspective because Trinidad was a small, white-dominated colony on the periphery of the British empire. There are no clues that explain his decision. Perhaps he yielded to pressure from his family to give up his itinerant ways, and he felt that there was less opportunity and temptation to travel about from a Trinidad base. There was doubtless the added attraction of returning to relatives and friends of long standing.

NOTES

1. T. McCants Stewart, *Liberia, The American-African Republic* (New York: E. O. Jenkins, 1886), p. 44.
2. *Crisis* (June 1923): 71, 72.
3. *Jamaican,* September 28, 1907.
4. Ibid.
5. "Affairs in Liberia," *Senate Documents,* vol. 60, 61st Cong., 2d sess., 1910.
6. *Jamaican,* September 28, 1907.
7. Document, Williams Papers, Barataria, Trinidad.
8. Republic of Liberia, Constitution, Article V, Section 12.
9. Article V, section 13 of the Constitution of Liberia of July 26, 1847. See George W. Brown, *Economic History of Liberia* (Washington, D.C.: Associated Publishers, 1941), p. 256. In the constitution as amended through May 1955, only "Negroes or persons of Negro descent" are eligible. Lawrence A. Marinelli, *New Liberia* (New York: Praeger, 1964), pp. 156, 157.

10. Wallis to Grey, February 11, 13, and 25, 1908, F.O. 367/85. Public Record Office, England.

11. Ibid., February 11, 1908, F.O. 367/85.

12. Marinelli, *New Liberia*, p. 42.

13. "Affairs in Liberia,", *Senate Documents.*

14. Wallis to Grey, February 11, 1908, F.O. 367/85.

15. Ibid., February 13, 1908, F.O. 367/85.

16. T. McCants Stewart, "New International Diplomacy and Practice," in *Second Annual Meeting of the Liberian Bar Association* (1908), p. 45.

17. H. S. Williams, "The Object of a Bar Association," in *Second Annual Meeting*, pp. 11-22.

18. A. J. Garvey, *Garvey and Garveyism* (Kingston, Jamaica, 1963), p. 63, citing New York newspaper reports of Du Bois's repudiation.

19. This appears to be an adaptation of verses from Walter Scott, *Lay of the Last Minstrel:*
> Breathes there the man with soul so dead
> Who never to himself hath said
> This is my own, my native land.

20. Affidavit of James Lionel Harris, appended to Wallis to Grey, February 25, 1908, F.O. 367/85.

21. Wallis to Grey, February 25, 1908, F.O. 367/85.

22. Wallis to Grey, February 25, 1908, F.O. 367/85.

23. Harry Dean, *The Pedro Gorino: The Adventures of a Negro Sea-Captain in Africa* (Boston: Houghton Mifflin, 1929), p. 119.

24. Wallis to Grey, February 25, 1908, F.O. 367/85.

25. "Affairs in Liberia," *Senate Documents.*

26. Ibid., p. 19.

27. Hollis R. Lynch, *Edward Wilmot Blyden, Pan-Negro Patriot* (London and New York: Oxford University Press, 1967), p. 71.

28. *Port-of-Spain Gazette,* October 30, 1909.

29. Gwendolen M. Carter, ed., *African One-Party States* (Ithaca, N.Y.: Cornell University Press, 1962), pp. 91-92. See also Irving L. Maskowitz, "The Political Thought of Blaise Diagne and Lamine Gueye," *Présence Africaine* 72 (1969): 25, and *Crisis* (April 1919): 274.

30. Interview with Mr. H. F. Sylvester Williams, Trinidad, November 1968.

31. John Thomas to Williams, April 27, 1908, Williams Papers.

32. D. D. T. Jabavu, *Life of John Tengo Jabavu* (Lovedale, South Africa: Lovedale Institution Press, 1922), p. 71.

Home to Trinidad: 11
Final Years

Williams traveled to Trinidad with his family from England on the
steamship *Salybia* and arrived in Port-of-Spain on August 29, 1908.
Two days later he was admitted to the bar and welcomed by Chief
Justice Lucie-Smith.[1] The Trinidad bar had a high reputation for the
skill of its members, among whom there was keen competition. The
barristers were mainly black and colored Trinidadians, the judges all
English.

Among the barristers in practice were some of Williams's colleagues
of Gray's Inn days—R. E. Phipps and E. A. Durham, both of the
African Association, and Charles S. René of the deputation to the Liberal MPs in the House of Commons in 1899. There were also the reformers Henry Alcazar and Prudhomme David, who had become the
first black member of the Trinidad Legislative Council in 1904. Among
the solicitors were Williams's friend Lazare and Eugene Bernard Acham
(the Afro-Chinese who was to become famous as Eugene Chen,[2] foreign minister of China) and his brother David Acham.

Williams settled down to his law practice in Port-of-Spain. He also
had a clerk in San Fernando and traveled to rural courts on the respective court days. But he found time to deliver a lecture in Sangre
Grande in early November. Perhaps the topic, "Liberia," was suggested by the sponsors, showing their interest in Africa was still strong.
Only eight months earlier he had said in his address to the Liberian
National Bar Association that some of his friends in the West Indies
had charged him with a mission to "enlighten them on practical
possibilities" in Liberia because they wished to settle there. Perhaps
some of these now wanted a firsthand report.

In the lecture he did not depart much from the recommendations
in his newsletter to the *Jamaican* that rather than go to the Latin

American republics they should go and help build Liberia and become citizens immediately and feel at home among their own kind. He spoke on the basis of personal observation. He doubtless emphasized the difference in the forms of government. Trinidad was the colony of a white European power where the people, the majority of them black, elected no one to represent them on the governing council although they paid the bulk of the taxes. Liberia was an independent state of black people who elected their president, their Senate, and their House of Representatives consisting of Africans like themselves. Liberia was the fulfillment of his dictum, "No one can represent the Negro but a Negro." [3]

It must have been particularly trying for Williams that in Trinidad there was still no avenue for public expression of the people's will. Despite all the efforts of the reformers, which he had supported from London, the legislature was still not representative and Port-of-Spain was still without a municipal council. Rostant had died, the crown colony system was still in existence, and the people remained to be enfranchised. Williams had been a municipal councillor in London and had aspired to be elected to Parliament, yet in his own home he could not seek the suffrages of his people.

Williams had been deeply touched, soon after his return to London from South Africa, to hear of Maresse-Smith's death in 1905. He had vowed then that whenever he returned home he would mention Edgar's name the very first time he spoke in public. This he did when he attended a meeting at the Victoria Institute in September 1909 to support the affirmative side in a debate on the topic, "The custom of standing drinks is a social evil." [4] Apparently his temperance reputation was still well remembered.

The Victoria Institute, established as a memorial to the queen after her golden jubilee in 1887, was the mecca of the young men of Port-of-Spain—the ambitious, forward-looking ones, teachers, law clerks aspiring to be solicitors, pharmacy students, store clerks, all desirous of practicing public speaking and cultivating their minds. It was more the presence of Williams than the topic that drew an audience that filled the hall, leading the *Gazette* to observe that there had not been such a large gathering since the "memorable occasion" when Bishop Hayes spoke on "Mens Sana in Corpore Sano," Attorney-General Nathan on "Correct Speaking and Thinking," and Sir Hugh Clifford, colonial secretary, on "Imperialism." The meeting was chaired by Lewis Inniss, a druggist, president of the institute's debating section, and later the author of *Trinidad and Trinidadians* (1910). Williams recalled, with the great approval of the audience, Maresse-Smith's dedicated struggle for social and political reform in Trinidad, and he suggested that there should be "some tangible memorial, however modest," in Maresse-Smith's honor. Williams himself took the lead in raising funds for this purpose. And so, on Sunday, October 3, 1909, a tombstone of blue marble was unveiled over the grave in the Lapeyrouse Cemetery, Port-of-Spain, with the simple inscription "EDGAR MARESSE-SMITH." Williams attended the ceremony with his wife. Some of the others, including Mr. and Mrs. Lazare, brought wreaths. One wreath bore the inscription, "The Trinidad Workingmen's Association Incorporated. In loving memory of Mr. E. L. Maresse-Smith. He wrought his people lasting good. R.I.P." The newspaper report of the unveiling correctly pointed out that "it is entirely due to his [Williams's] energy and push that a tombstone is today erected over the grave of a man whose memory Trinidad reveres." [5]

Williams lived a quiet home life between the time of his return to Trinidad and his death. Being a teetotaler, he did not frequent the Ice House Hotel where the more outgoing lawyers gathered in the evening. He went straight home from his chambers to his family. Young Henry attended Queen's Royal College and no longer worried about having to fight on being called a "blackamoor," as he was by the white boys of Marylebone Grammar School in London. He was his father's companion; they were often in conversation and his mother would remark that Father treated the youngster like a man. Father had taught him chess and they sometimes played. At other times young Henry would read to him from Stead's *Review of Reviews,* from the volumes of *Library of Famous Literature,* which he had brought from England, or from the local newspapers. Sometimes the family—there were also the small ones, Elizabeth Irene, Charles, and Agnes— would gather around the piano and sing, with Father or Mother playing and sometimes Henry, whom Mother had taught.

In addition to his practice, Williams made an unsuccessful venture in the ownership of two sailing vessels that traded between Venezuelan ports and Port-of-Spain. One was seized in a Venezuelan port and the other holed and sunk. At the subsequent sale the hulk fetched only a negligible sum. [6]

Williams maintained a keen interest in public affairs. He was a main speaker at a special meeting of the Workingmen's Association on October 29, 1909, called to discuss the restoration of municipal government, and he attended the opening of the new session of the Legislative Council. His relationship with the Workingmen's Association was frowned upon by local officials and the employer class; they saw it as a challenge to their continued domination. At the meeting Williams disclosed that before he came to the meeting he had been advised that he should be careful about identifying himself with labor—but he had not been deterred. The association had been formed in 1896 by Hamel-Smith and others.[7] In the climate of crown colony rule, the operation of an organization that sought to protect the rights of workers proved to be a difficult task, and the association declined. It was revived in 1906 under the presidency of an Afro-Chinese druggist, Alfred Richards, who had joined in welcoming Williams on his visit home in 1901. Following its revival, the association had forged strong links with the labor movement in England and, according to a letter from Keir Hardie read at an earlier meeting, the association was "the only organization outside Great Britain which is affiliated to the Labour Party."[8] In view of Williams's links with Keir Hardie and the other Labour MPs, it is conceivable that he was instrumental in arranging the connection.

Along with the members, mainly clerks, artisans, and port workers, at the special meeting were several lawyers, including Lazare and Grecian Donawa, who had been chairman of the Princes Town branch of the Pan-African Association and secretary of the Canefarmers' Association. Williams complained that the British were backward in recognizing the ability of black men. He advised that branches of the association should be established throughout the country and special meetings held regularly to discuss their problems. He argued that Port-of-Spain, which had one of the best informed and most progressive populations in the British empire, fully deserved an elected municipal council.

Williams was evidently looking forward to the day when he could serve as a borough councillor of Port-of-Spain and perhaps as a member of the Legislative Council, but it was not until seventeen months after his death that the municipality was restored and another twelve years before a restricted legislative franchise was conceded to his fellow countrymen. They were yet a long way from the representative government he had advocated in 1899. The Workingmen's Association received a well-merited reward for its interest in the restoration of municipal government when its President Richards—like Bass of the Pan-African Association before him—eventually became mayor of Port-of-Spain.

Williams was "among the general audience" at the opening of the Legislative Council on November 3, 1909. The governor, Sir George Le Hunte, painted a bleak, disquieting picture of economic conditions. He spoke of "the scarcity of money in circulation caused partly by the low prices of our principal products," of business being at a "standstill," of the more energetic of the laboring classes seeking employment elsewhere, with those remaining being "in a condition of restless discontent," of the high death rate of infants and of too widespread disease like consumption and "the plague." Like his friends in the Workingmen's Association, Williams must have been disturbed by these conditions and by the increased customs duties that the governor proposed.

Williams and his wife were present at the Arouca Presbyterian Church on July 16, 1910, to join a ceremony for the Rev. W. F. Dickson to mark the end of his forty-eight years of service to the community. Dickson, who had years earlier been chairmen of the Pan-African Association branch at Arouca, was to outlive his younger friend by two months.

Williams's practice at the bar was growing steadily. He was busy in the Supreme Court in civil cases and appeals and at criminal sessions both in Port-of-Spain and in San Fernando. Justice Russell, whom he often appeared before, considered him "extremely successful" in his practice. For instance, on successive days at San Fernando Assizes in October 1909, he secured the acquittal of an Indian man on a perjury charge—a "perplexing case," the judge called it—and of another man held on a wounding charge. In the second case he had intervened during the hearing and asked Justice Russell to permit him to assist the prisoner.

By late 1910 Williams was struck down by a severe kidney ailment. He never recovered completely, though he was able to go to his chambers on a few occasions. He died in a hospital on March 26, 1911.[9] Earlier in the day his son Henry had been at his bedside reading the newspaper to him.

There were the usual kindly references in the courts, by judges, magistrates, barristers, and solicitors, to a lawyer's passing. Chief Justice Lucie-Smith recalled Williams's courtesy and said his death would be a loss to the bar. Justice Russell disclosed his feeling of high regard for Williams, who had left a wife and four children.[10] The fifth—a boy— was born five days after his father's death.

NOTES

1. *Mirror,* September 3, 1908.

2. In Chinese, Ch'en Yu-jen, according to the *Biographical Dictionary of Republican China,* Vol. 1 (New York: Columbia University Press, 1967), pp. 180-183. Chen wrote Sun Yat-Sen's farewell message to the Soviet Union.

3. *Pan-African* (October 1901): 1.

4. *Port-of-Spain Gazette,* September 18, 1909.

5. *Mirror,* October 5, 1909.

6. Conversations with Mr. H. F. Sylvester Williams in Trinidad, November 1968.

7. *Reform,* September 26, 1896.

8. *Port-of-Spain Gazette,* October 29, 1909.

9. Records of Registrar-General's Department, Port-of-Spain, show the cause of death as "chronic nephritis."

10. *Mirror,* March 28, 1911; *Port-of-Spain Gazette,* March 28, 1911.

Conclusion   12

It now remains to view Williams and his contributions within the
context of the history of the Pan-African idea and movement, for
Williams had been consigned to near obscurity by writers on pan-Africanism, including W. E. B. Du Bois and George Padmore who, while
carrying on the movement, credited him merely with the invention of
the term "Pan-African" in calling the Pan-African Conference in London
in 1900. They knew or said little about Williams and his contribution
to pan-Africanism either before or after the conference.

To be sure, the Pan-African idea—the concept of black race pride,
solidarity, and initiative in the face of white exploitation and domination—long predates Williams, going back at least to the early nineteenth century.[1] Its earliest exponents were frustrated and race-proud
members of the westernized black elite in the Americas and somewhat
later in West Africa. Among the predecessors of Williams as Pan-African
spokesmen were such Afro-Americans as Paul Cuffee, John B. Russwurm,
Martin R. Delany, Alexander Crummell, Bishop James T. Holly, and
Bishop Henry McNeal Turner, and, in West Africa, Edward Wilmot
Blyden, James Africanus Beale Horton, and James Johnson.[2] But it
can be argued that Williams was the first pan-Africanist, not only because he invented and gave currency to the term "Pan-African" but
also because more than any of his predecessors or contemporaries, he
strove to give organizational form to the idea. Indeed, in the history of
pan-Africanism, Williams's concern for the establishment of local
branches of the Pan-African Association throughout the black world
was emulated and surpassed only by Marcus Garvey and his Universal
Negro Improvement Association.

Among major contemporary advocates of pan-Africanism, Williams
met and conferred with at least three of them—Bishops Turner and Holly

and James Johnson. Although there is as yet no concrete evidence, it seems probable that Williams also met Blyden. Williams was in London during Blyden's brief posting in the summer of 1905 as the Liberian minister to London and Paris. And during Williams's eventful visit to Liberia in 1908, Blyden was in the black republic. At any rate, among the leading early race-conscious black intellectuals, it was the ideas of Blyden, easily the foremost pan-African ideologue of his time, which seemed to have had the greatest influence on Williams. Rev. Philip Douglin, a friend of Williams while he was still a young man, had spent a long time as a missionary in the Rio Pongo close to the fields of Blyden's endeavors in Liberia and Sierra Leone, and doubtless he spoke about the West Indian-born Liberian. But there is other evidence that Blyden's influence had spread to Trinidad. J. J. Thomas had read Blyden's writings and mentions him, along with Alexander Crummell, in his book.[3] And there is telling evidence of Blyden's profound influence on Trinidadians of Williams's age group and background in Frederick Alexander Durham's *The Lone Star of Liberia* (1892) in the introduction to which the young author exultantly praised Blyden and expressed the hope that his own work was not "an unsuitable appendix or supplement" to Blyden's major work, *Christianity, Islam and the Negro Race* (1887), which he recommended as compulsory reading for all black people interested in the history of their race. Interestingly, Marcus Garvey was to make a similar appeal before leaving Jamaica for the United States. [4]

There can be no doubt that Williams was familiar with and adopted some of Blyden's views. Like Blyden, he saw Liberia as potentially an important Pan-African base and he viewed European missionary activities in Africa as permeated with sectarianism, cultural ethnocentrism, and other arrogant forms of alleged European superiority, producing divisions, dislocations, and a sense of inferiority among their African protégés. And just as Blyden worked toward a nonsectarian West African Christian church that would accommodate itself to basic African mores and customs, so Williams had supported the idea of an independent African church in South Africa. But Williams, who himself would have qualified as "pure black," never accepted Blyden's obsessive anti-mulatto ideas or any other racist position.

Williams would undoubtedly have invited Blyden to the Pan-African Conference since he was the leading Pan-African intellectual of his time. Indeed, the brilliant Blyden would have been a star attraction.

But Blyden did not attend. His biographer has speculated that he would have been opposed to the conference on the grounds that it was being held in a European rather than an African venue and that mulattoes were permitted to participate. [5] At any rate, he would have had difficulty in getting to London because he had recently rejoined the faculty of Liberia College and was pressed for both time and money.

Whether or not they met in Liberia in 1908, they were on opposing sides of a central current issue for the black republic: how in the face of European imperial designs on it Liberia could survive and progress. Williams talked in terms of getting West Indians to come to the aid of the embattled nation, while Blyden favored a temporary British protectorate.

Even after Williams finally left for Trinidad in 1908, his influence in Britain persisted. This can best be seen in the works of Duse Mohammed Ali, a Sudanese-Egyptian, and F. E. M. Hercules, a fellow West Indian. In July 1912, Mohammed Ali founded the *African Times and Orient Review* with the backing of a black businessman, J. Eldred Taylor. *The Review* became the chief propagator of pan-African thinking during the seven years of its existence. Mohammed Ali had lived in England for several years and his monthly *Review* not only used the term "Pan-African" but showed awareness of Williams's ideas and activities. The office of Mohammed Ali's newspaper became a regular meeting place for Pan-Africanists and anticolonial agitators from Asia, Africa, and the West Indies. Between 1912 and 1914, the young Marcus Garvey, while still forging his pan-African views, worked for Mohammed Ali's paper. Interestingly, Duse himself was to work for Marcus Garvey's *Negro World* on his visit to New York in the early 1920s before going on to Nigeria where he became involved in the developing nationalist movement.

Hercules, too, was a contributor to Mohammed Ali's paper and in other ways helped to develop pan-African consciousness among blacks. Hercules may be said to have donned Williams's mantle as a spokesman for blacks in Britain. He was thirteen years old when Williams visited Trinidad in 1901 and was still attending Queen's Royal College, Trinidad's premier secondary school, when he formed a Young Men's Colored Association. Moving to London around 1914 or 1915 to complete his academic studies, he eventually became editor of the

monthly *African Telegraph* under Taylor's ownership, which was launched in December 1918, just about the time of the closure of the *Afri-*
can Times and Orient Review.

The *Telegraph* served as the organ of the Society of Peoples of
African Origin, which Hercules founded, with Taylor as chairman and
himself as general secretary, with the object of fostering black unity,
bringing grievances to public notice, and promoting closer commercial
ties between Britain and its African and West Indian colonies. Taylor
also formed the African Cooperative Corporation to promote economic
development in West Africa.

Hercules was in the forefront of protest against racial discrimination
and ill-treatment of black West Indian World War I veterans in England,
which culminated in serious antiblack riots in 1918 and 1919. The
paper closed while Hercules, after the fashion of Williams, was on a
Caribbean lecture tour, which took him to Jamaica, Trinidad, and British Guiana (now Guyana) and ended in the United States where the last
was heard of him. [6] The effects of his lectures in a time of serious labor
unrest among black workers in the West Indies, where Garvey's UNIA
had branches and the influence of his propaganda in New York was
being felt, led the Colonial Office to conclude that Hercules's aim was
the "ultimate independence of negro countries" though he was content
with their remaining under British rule for the time being. [7] Like-
wise, Garvey's *Negro World* was banned in several colonies as a "seditious publication" under new laws making the importation or possession of it punishable by fine and imprisonment.

If, like Garvey, Williams emphasized the organization of local
Pan-African branches in the various parts of the black world, it is
also true that the Pan-African Conference he organized in 1900 remained essentially the model for the later Pan-African conferences,
first organized by W. E. B. Du Bois and later by George Padmore and
Kwame Nkrumah, who became the leading organizer of these conferences. [8] This Pan-African Conference movement was to culminate
first in the All Africa Peoples Conference in Accra in 1958 and in 1963
in the formation of the Organization of African Unity, pledged to
foster cooperation between African states and people and to rid the
continent of European colonialism and domination. Thus, although
neither scholars nor black nationalists have acclaimed Williams, there

is no doubt that he is a significant and central figure in the struggles
of black people everywhere to achieve freedom, dignity, and self-
expression.

NOTES

1. See Hollis R. Lynch, "Pan-Negro Nationalism in the New World
Before 1862," *Boston University Papers on Africa*, ed. Jeffrey Butler
(Boston: Boston University Press, 1966), 2: 149-79.

2. See Edwin Redkey, *Black Exodus: Black Nationalist and Back-to-
Africa Movement, 1890-1910* (New Haven: Yale University Press,
1969), and Robert July, *The Origins of Modern West African Thought*
(New York: Praeger, 1968), passim.

3. J. J. Thomas, *Froudacity* (1889; reprint ed., London: New Beacon
Books, 1969), p. 192.

4. Marcus Garvey, *A Talk with Afro-West Indians* (Kingston, 1916?),
reprinted in John Henrik Clarke, *Garvey and the Vision of Africa* (New
York: Vintage Press, 1974), pp. 83-87. Garvey wrote in part: "You who
do not know anything of your ancestry will do well to read the works
of Blyden."

5. Hollis R. Lynch, *Edward W. Blyden, Pan-Negro Patriot, 1832-1912*
(London and New York: Oxford University Press, 1967), pp. 250-251.

6. See W. F. Elkins, "Hercules and the Society of Peoples of African
Origin," *Caribbean Studies* 2 (January 1972): 47-49. Hercules was not
allowed to land in Trinidad because, according to the governor, he was
"a native of British Guiana" and "in view of the excitement prevailing" his
"presence might endanger the public safety." Reply to question in British
House of Commons, March 2, 1920, in Despatches from Secretary of
State, 1920, Vol. II (Minute 2617 transmitting questions and answers
in Parliament for period ending March 11, 1920), in Trinidad and
Tobago Archives).

7. Telegram, Colonial Secretary to Governor of Jamaica, August 15,
1919, PRO, C.O. 318/351, Public Record Office.

8. See Vincent B. Thompson, *Africa and Unity: The Evolution
of Pan-Africanism* (New York: Humanities Press, 1969), chap. 1.

Appendix: Who Was Who at the 1900 Pan-African Conference

Alcindor, Dr. John. Believed to have come from the West Indies, probably Trinidad; was still in London in 1923 when he took part in Du Bois's Pan-African Congress.

Archer, John R. Medical student who became photographer; son of Barbadian father and Irish mother; later mayor of London borough of Battersea; correspondent of well-known Afro-American journalist, John E. Bruce ("Bruce Grit"), who wrote introduction to Bishop Walters's *My Life and Work;* attended Pan-African Congress, Paris, 1919.

Arnett, Chaplain Benjamin W., Jr. Of Illinois; son of Bishop Benjamin W. Arnett, of AME church, chaplain of regiment of U. S. volunteers in Spanish-American War.

Brown, Reverend Henry B. Of London, Ontario, Canada; probably Henry "Box" Brown who, as a slave in the South, so resented separation from wife and children that he arranged with friendly white merchant to be shipped in crate by rail, steamship, and wagon to Philadelphia and freedom, and later to a career as an antislavery lecturer.

Calloway, Professor Thomas J. Hampton Institute, Hampton, Virginia; supervisor of American Negro exhibit at Paris exposition, 1900.

Christian, George James. 1869-1940; law student from Dominica, West Indies; educated at Dominica Grammar School; former teacher; called to the bar by Gray's Inn; later settled in Gold Coast; twice member, Sekondi Town Council; member, Legislative Council, 1920-1940.

Cooper, Mrs. Anna J. Teacher of Latin, Washington, D.C., high school; author of *A Voice from the South* (1892).

Dove, G. W. Member, municipal council, Freetown, Sierra Leone.

Downing, Henry Francis. b. 1851; former United States consul, São Paulo de Loanda, Portuguese Africa; author of *Liberia and Her People* (1925), *The American Cavalryman* (1917), and *The Tangle* (1919).

Du Bois, Dr. William Edward Burghardt. 1868-1963; professor of economics and history, Atlanta University; educated at Fisk University, University of Berlin, and Harvard University (Ph.D., 1895). Author of three publications at time of conference: *The Suppression of the African Slave Trade* (1896), *The Philadelphia Negro* (1899), and *The Conservation of Races* (1897), Occasional Paper No. 2 of the American Negro Academy, of which he was a founding member. One of the founders of the Niagara movement (1905-1909), out of which grew the National Association for the Advancement of Colored People; director of publicity and research, NAACP, editor of *Crisis,* organ of NAACP, 1910-1934; organizer of Pan-African Congresses 1919, 1921, and 1923; presided over Pan-African Congress, Manchester, England, 1945; U.S. Special Minister Plenipotentiary and Envoy Extraordinary to inauguration of President C. D. B. King of Liberia, 1923; editor of *Phylon* and author of many books; died in Ghana, aged ninety-five, having taken Ghanaian citizenship and joined the American Communist party.

French, C. W. Of St. Kitts.

Hamilton, A. R. Of Jamaica. Mentioned in Walters's list of delegates and in conference report for services rendered; signatory to Bishop Johnson's address.

Harris, Miss Ada. Of Indiana.

Johnson, Frederick E. R. Former attorney-general of Liberia; later secretary of state; son and grandson of former presidents of Liberia; visited London in 1907 in suite of President Barclay, who invited Williams to Liberia.

Jones, Miss Anna M.A., Teacher in Kansas City High School; alumna of University of Michigan; described in *New Negro for a New Century* (1900) as a brilliant linguist and teacher.

Joseph, Reverend Henry Mason. From Antigua; formerly headmaster, St. Joseph's High School, St. John's, Antigua; president, African Association and Pan-African Conference Committee.

Lee, Charles P. Attorney, of Rochester, New York.

Loudin, Mr. and Mrs. John F. He was manager, Fisk Jubilee Singers.

Love, Professor John L. Teacher in Colored High School, Washington, D.C., and member, American Negro Academy; author of Academy Occasional Paper, *The Disfranchisement of the Negro* (1899); secretary, Pan-African Conference, 1900.

Meyer, William Henry. Medical student from Trinidad; delegate (with Savage) of Afro-West Indian Literary Society of Edinburgh; returned to Trinidad 1902 as supernumerary medical officer in government service.

Moschelles, Mr. and Mrs. Felix. Contributed to Pan-African funds and spoke at conference; country of origin is unknown but possibly Cape Colony.

Phipps, Richard E. Barrister-at-law; returned to Trinidad immediately after conference; left Trinidad shortly after Williams's death there in 1911 and settled in Gold Coast; died there about 1926.

Pierre, Alexander Pulcherie. Of Trinidad; founder of Trinidad Literary Association, 1887; signatory of reform petition, 1886; law student.

Quinlan, John Ephraim. Sworn land surveyor, St. Lucia; subsequently lived in England; with D. E. Tobias, opposed recruitment of labor from West Indies for South African mines at joint meeting of Anti-Slavery Society and Aborigines Protection Society, Caxton Hall, London, April 29, 1903.

Ribeiro, Miguel Francisco. Barrister-at-law of Lincoln's Inn; from Gold Coast.

Roberts, Mrs. Jane. Mentioned by Williams as having a position on the platform; widow of first president of Liberia, James Jenkins Roberts; last survivor of early Liberian settlers.

Savage, Dr. R. A. K. Of Gold Coast; one of two delegates from Afro-West Indian Literary Society of Edinburgh, Scotland; listed in conference report as secretary for Abyssinia though it is not clear why he is linked with Abyssinia; later editor, *Gold Coast Leader,* described as journalistic vehicle of patriot Joseph E. Casely Hayford (1886-1930), with whom he is said to have discussed idea of united action among people of West Africa.

Smith, Reverend Henry. Of London, England; later chosen vice-president, Pan-African Association.

Solomon, Reverend S. R. B.(Attoh-Ahuma). Mentioned twice by Williams as having arrived for the conference but not mentioned in connection with conference proceedings; of Gold Coast.

Straker, Judge David Augustus. 1842-1908; of Michigan; mentioned by Benito Sylvain as a delegate; was one of the leading men consulted by Williams before the conference; author of *The New South Investigated* (1888), *Reflections on the Life and Times of Toussaint L'Ouverture* (1886), and *A Trip to the Windward Islands or Then and Now* (1896).

Sylvain, Benito. b. 1868; Haitian aide-de-camp to Emperor Menelik II of Abyssinia; elected general delegate for Africa on executive of Pan-African Association; journalist and former secretary, Haitian legation, London, and Envoy Extraordinary for Haiti to the court of Emperor Menelik; editor, *La Fraternité*, Paris, 1890-1893, *L'Étoile Africaine;* author, *Du Sort des Indigènes dans les Colonies d'Exploitation* (1901) containing chapter on Pan-African Conference, 1900; later Docteur-en-Droit, Faculté de Paris, and commander, Haitian marines.

Taylor, Samuel Coleridge. Musician, composer of "Hiawatha's Wedding Feast"; son of Sierra Leone father and English mother; born and resident in London; mentioned by Du Bois in essay in *Darkwater.*

Tobias, D. E. b. circa 1870, native of South Carolina; studied prison system in England; illiterate until fourteen, then largely self-educated; author of "A Negro on the Position of the Negro in America," in *The Nineteenth Century,* London (December 1899), and also a pamphlet, *Freed, But Not Free* (n.d.), on convict lease system.

Walters, Bishop Alexander. 1858-1917; leader in the American Methodist Episcopal Zion church in the United States; prominent in the World Christian Endeavor Movement; president of the National Afro-American Council; early member of the board of the National Association for the Advancement of Colored People; author of *My Life and Work* (1917), in which he describes the Pan-African Conference over which he presided.

Williams, Mrs. Fannie Barrier. Prominent newspaper correspondent, social worker, and club woman of Chicago, Illinois; author of

"The Club Movement Among Colored Women of America," in Booker T. Washington's *A New Negro for a New Century* (1900).

Williams, H. S. 1869-1911; of Trinidad; convener of the conference, founder of African Association.

Worrell, J. W. D. Of Barbados; mentioned in conference report for "constant material support," but not mentioned as a delegate; signatory to Bishop Johnson's address.

OTHER PARTICIPANTS AND OBSERVERS AT THE 1900 PAN-AFRICAN CONFERENCE

Adams, Miss. Mentioned only by Sylvain as coming from Ireland; her name appears as a contributor to the conference fund.

Battersby, Harford. Secretary, Committee for Abolition of Native Liquor Traffic.

Bourne, H. R. Fox. Secretary, Aborigines Protection Society, and honorary member, African Association.

Buckle, J. Fellow, Royal Geographical Society.

Buxton, Sir T. Fowell. President, Anti-Slavery Society.

Clark, Dr. Gavin. Liberal MP.

Cobden-Unwin, Mrs. Jessie. Wife of publisher T. Fisher Unwin; praised by Booker T. Washington in *Up from Slavery* for hospitality during London visit, 1899; elected to executive committee, Pan-African Association.

Colenso, Dr. R. J. Son of Bishop Colenso of Natal; elected general treasurer at Pan-African Conference but not mentioned as a delegate.

Creighton, Dr. Mandell. 1843-1901; bishop of London.

Ware, Francis. Mentioned by Walters as one of the speakers at the conference, but his name is not found elsewhere.

Bibliography

MANUSCRIPTS

The manuscript sources on Henry Sylvester Williams are scant; there are only a relatively few items in those listed below.

The Williams Papers. In possession of Williams's eldest son, Henry Francis Sylvester Williams of Barataria, Trinidad.

The papers include two letters by Williams to his wife. One seems to be the first he ever wrote to her; the other his second from South Africa. There are a few letters to Williams: one each from Charles Duncan, MP, secretary of the Workers' Union, and Emmanuel Mzumbo Lazare, Trinidad lawyer and nationalist, and three and part of a fourth from Sir Henri Gustave Joly de Lotbinière, a high French Canadian government official. The papers also include Williams's certificates obtained as a barrister in England and as an advocate in Cape Colony; a deed of lease of land in Liberia; a leaflet on the League of Universal Brotherhood and Native Races Association; a few clippings from *South Africa, John Bull Overseas,* and the *Daily Express* dealing with the visit of the Basuto chiefs to London, one of a letter to the *Leader* from Williams appealing to "my white brothers" for humane treatment of his "fellow countrymen" in Africa, one from the *Rochester, Chatham and Gillingham Journal* containing the obituary of Williams's father-in-law, Major Francis Powell, and a clipping from the *Jamaican* of a newsletter written by Williams reporting an interview with President Arthur Barclay of Liberia in London and advocating the emigration of West Indians to Liberia.

The Anti-Slavery Papers. Rhodes House Library, Oxford.

A few letters Williams wrote between 1899 and 1901 to the secretary of the British and Foreign Anti-Slavery Society and the replies to Williams. Other relevant materials are the prospectus of Wooding's Preparatory Private School, Cape Town, and minutes of the Anti-Slavery Society.

F.O. 367/85. Public Record Office, London.

Three dispatches from Captain C. Braithwaite Wallis, British consul at Monrovia, to Lord Grey, the British Foreign Secretary.

South Africa: A Collection of Miscellaneous Documents (microfilm), Hoover Institution, Stanford.

In reel 7 Williams is referred to in two letters from John Tengo Jabavu to John Tobin in the Tobin Papers; and, there is a report from the *Owl* of Williams's speech at his first public meeting. Reel 11 contains Lionel Forman's pamphlet, *Chapters in the History of South Africa's March to Freedom,* which has important information on various personalities in colored politics at the turn of the century.

John E. Bruce Papers. Schomburg Collection, New York Public Library, Harlem.

Du Bois Papers. Accra, Ghana.

This contains the only extant copy of the report of the Pan-African Conference (1900).

NEWSPAPERS

African Times and Orient Review.
Cape Argus (Cape Town).
Cape Times (Cape Town).
Chicago Defender.
Christian Express (Cape Town).
Colored American (Washington, D.C.).
Creole Bitters (Port-of-Spain).
Daily Express (London).
Daily Gleaner (Kingston).
Daily News (Port-of-Spain).
Jamaica Advocate (Kingston).
Jamaica Times (Kingston).

Lagos Chronicle.
Lagos Standard.
Leader (London).
Marylebone Mercury (London).
Mirror (Port-of-Spain).
Morning Post (London).
New Age (London).
New Era (Port-of-Spain).
New York Age (New York City).
Pall Mall Gazette.
Port-of-Spain Gazette.
Public Opinion (Port-of-Spain).
Reform (Port-of-Spain).
San Fernando Gazette.
Times (London).
The Truth (Port-of-Spain).
West London Gazette.

JOURNALS

Aborigines Friend (London).
African Repository (Washington, D.C.).
Anti-Slavery Reporter (London).
Bulletin de la Société de Géographie de Toulouse (Toulouse).
Crisis (New York City).
L'Etoile Africaine (Paris).
John Bull Overseas (London).
Liberia Bulletin (Washington, D.C.).
Pan-African (London).
Présence Africaine (Paris).
Review of Reviews (London).
South Africa (London).

WRITINGS OF HENRY SYLVESTER WILLIAMS

The British Negro: A Factor in the Empire. London, 1902.
"The Object of a Bar Association." In *Second Annual Meeting of the Liberian National Bar Association in the Executive Mansion, Monrovia, February 5, 1908.* Monrovia: College of West Africa Press, 1908.

"Trinidad, B.W.I." In *British America.* British Empire Series, vol. 3. London: Kegan Paul, Trench, Trubner & Co. Ltd, 1900.

UNPUBLISHED DISSERTATIONS

Contee, Clarence. "W. E. B. DuBois and African Nationalism, 1914-1945." Ph.D. dissertation, The American University, 1969.

Duffield, Ian. "Duse Mohammed Ali." Ph.D. dissertation, University of Edinburgh, 1972.

Johnson, H. B. D. "Crown Colony Government in Trinidad and Tobago, 1870-1897." D. Phil. dissertation, Oxford University, 1969.

Samaroo, Brinsley. "Political and Constitutional Change in Trinidad, 1898-1925." Ph.D. dissertation, London University, 1969.

PRIMARY AND CONTEMPORARY WORKS

Attoh-Ahuma. *Memoirs of West African Celebrities.* Liverpool: D. Marples, 1905.

———.*The Gold Coast Nation and National Consciousness.* Liverpool: D. Marples, 1911.

Barrow, A. H. *Fifty Years in West Africa: Being a Record of the West Indian Church on the Banks of the,Rio Pongo.* London: SPCK, 1900.

Biggar, Emerson. *Canada, A Memorial Volume.* London: E. Stanford, 1889.

Bodu, José. *Trinidadiana.* Port-of-Spain: Blondell, 1915.

Bowen, John W. E., ed. *Africa and the American Negro: Addresses and Proceedings of the Congress on Africa.* 1896. Reprint. Miami, Fla.: Mnemosyne Publishing Inc., 1969.

Brierly, J. N. "The Police and the Public." In *Trinidad and Tobago Year Book.* Port-of-Spain: Government Printer, 1901.

———. *Trinidad: Then and Now.* Port-of-Spain: Franklin Electric Printery, 1912.

Les Conférences antiesclavagistes libres, Bruxelles, 1891. Brussels: Imprimerie Populaire, 1892.

Coppin, Bishop L. J. *Observations of Persons and Things in South Africa, 1900-1904.* Philadelphia: AME Books Concern, n.d.

Crummell, Alexander. *Africa and America.* 1891. Reprint. New York: Negro Universities Press, 1969.

Dean, Captain Harry. *The Pedro Gorino: The Adventures of a Negro Sea-Captain in Africa and on the Seven Seas in His Attempt to Found an Ethiopian Empire.* Boston: Houghton Mifflin, 1929.

Douglass, Frederick. *Life and Times of Frederick Douglass.* New York: Macmillan, 1962.

Du Bois, W. E. B. *ABC of Color*. Berlin: Seven Seas Publishers, 1963.
———. *Autobiography of W. E. B. Du Bois*. New York: International Publishers, 1968.
———. *Conservation of Races*. 1897. Reprint. Occasional Papers No. 2 of the American Negro Academy. New York: Arno Press, 1969.
———. *Darkwater*. 1920. Reprint. New York: Schocken Press, 1969.
———. *Dusk of Dawn*. 1940. Reprint. New York: Schocken Press, 1968.
———. *The World and Africa*. New York: International Publishers, 1965.
Ferris, William H. *The African Abroad; or, His Evolution in Western Civilization*. New Haven: The Tuttle, Morehouse and Taylor Press, 1913. 2 vols.
Fitzpatrick, Kathleen. *Lady Henry Somerset*. Boston: Little, Brown, 1923.
Gandhi, M. K. *Autobiography: Story of My Experiments with Truth*. Washington: Public Affairs Press, 1954.
Greenidge, Joseph I. *Bohemian Sketches*. Port-of-Spain: Greenidge, 1937.
Hobson, J. A. *The Psychology of Jingoism*. London: J. Richards, 1901.
Inniss, Lewis Osborn. *Trinidad and Trinidadians*. Port-of-Spain: Mirror Printing Works, 1910.
Jabavu, D. D. T. *Life of John Tengo Jabavu*. Lovedale, South Africa: Lovedale Institution Press, 1922.
Keith, A. B. *Responsible Government in the Dominions*. Oxford: Clarendon Press, 1910.
Livingston, W. P. *Black Jamaica*. London: Sampson, Low, 1899.
Lynch, Hollis R., ed. *Black Spokesman: Selected Published Writings of Edward Wilmot Blyden*. New York: Humanities Press, 1970.
———, ed. *Selected Letters of Edward Wilmot Blyden*. London: Frank Cass, 1975. 2 vols.
Morel, E. D. *Black Man's Burden*. Manchester: National Labour Press, 1920.
Morton, Sarah E. *John Morton of Trinidad: Journals, Letters and Papers*. Toronto: Westminster Co., 1916.
Padmore, George, ed., *History of the Pan-African Congress*. 2d ed. London: Hammersmith Bookshop, 1963.
Redkey, Edwin S. *Respect Black: The Writings and Speeches of Henry McNeal Turner*. New York: Arno Press, 1971.
Report of the Pan-African Conference . . . at Westminster Town Hall. London: The Pan-African Association, 1900.
Stewart, T. McCants. *Liberia, The American-African Republic*. New York: E. O. Jenkins, 1886.

Sylvain, Benito. *Du Sort des Indigènes dans les Colonies d'Exploita-*
tion. Paris: Boyer, 1901.

Thomas, J. J. *Froudacity.* 1889. Reprint. London: New Beacon Books,
1969.

Walters, Alexander. *My Life and Work.* New York: Fleming H. Revell
Company, 1917.

Washington, Booker T., ed. *New Negro for a New Century.* Chicago:
American Publishing House, 1900.

Wells-Barnett, Ida. *On Lynching.* 1892. Reprint. New York: Arno Press,
1969.

SECONDARY WORKS

Books

AMSAC. *Pan-Africanism Reconsidered.* Berkeley: University of California Press, 1962.

Asiegbu, Johnson U. J. *Slavery and the Politics of Liberation, 1787-*
1861. London: Longmans, 1969.

Ayandele, E. A. *Holy Johnson: Pioneer of African Nationalism.* New
York: Humanities Press, 1970.

Bittle, William E., and Geis, Gilbert. *The Longest Way Home: Chief*
Alfred C. Sam's Back-to-Africa Movement. Detroit: Wayne State
University Press, 1964.

Brookes, Edgar H. *The Color Problems of South Africa.* London:
Paul, Trench, Trufer, 1934.

Brown, George. *An Economic History of Liberia.* Washington, D.C.:
Associated Publishers, 1941.

Buell, R. L. *Liberia: A Century of Survival, 1847-1947.* Philadelphia:
University of Pennsylvania Press, 1947.

Carmichael, Gertrude. *A History of the West Indian Islands of Trinidad*
and Tobago, 1498-1900. London: Redman, 1961.

Clarke, John H., ed. *Marcus Garvey and the Vision of Africa.* New
York: Random House, 1974.

Curtin, Philip D., ed. *Africa Remembered.* Madison: University of
Wisconsin Press, 1967.

Duplessis, J. *A History of Christian Missions in South Africa.* London:
Longmans, 1911.

Fuller, Frederick. *A Vanished Dynasty, Ashanti.* London: Murray, 1921.

Garvin, James L. *Life of Joseph Chamberlain.* London: Macmillan,
1934.

Geiss, Imanuel. *Panafrikanismus, Zur Geschichte Der Dekolonisation.* Frankfurt am Main: Europaische Verlagsanstalt, 1965.

Hamilton, Bruce. *Barbados and the Confederation Question, 1871-1885.* London: Crown Agents, 1956.

July, Robert W. *The Origins of Modern African Political Thought: Its Development in West Africa During the Nineteenth and Twentieth Century.* New York: Praeger, 1968.

Kellogg, Charles F. *N.A.A.C.P.* Baltimore: Johns Hopkins Press, 1967.

Langer, William L. *The Diplomacy of Imperialism, 1890-1902.* New York: Alfred Knopf, 1951.

Langley, J. Ayodele. *Pan-Africanism and Nationalism in West Africa, 1900-1945.* Oxford: Clarendon Press, 1973.

Logan, Rayford. *Diplomatic Relations of the United States with Haiti, 1776-1891.* Chapel Hill: University of North Carolina Press, 1941.

Lynch, Hollis R. *Edward Wilmot Blyden, Pan-Negro Patriot, 1832-1912.* London and New York: Oxford University Press, 1967.

Marais, J. S. *The Cape Coloured People, 1652-1937.* London: Longmans, 1939.

Marks, Shula. *Reluctant Rebellion: The 1906-08 Disturbances in Natal.* Oxford: Clarendon Press, 1970.

Padmore, George. *Pan-Africanism or Communism?* 1956. Reprint. Garden City, N.Y.: Doubleday, 1971.

Parry, J. H., and Sherlock, P. M. *A Short History of the West Indies.* London: Macmillan, 1957.

Redkey, Edwin S. *Black Exodus: Black Nationalist and Back-to-Africa Movements, 1890-1910.* New Haven: Yale University Press, 1969.

Roux, Edward. *Time Longer Than Rope: A History of the Struggle of the Black Man for Freedom in South Africa.* Madison: University of Wisconsin Press, 1964.

Rudwick, Elliott M. *W. E. B. Du Bois, A Study in Minority Race Leadership.* Philadelphia: University of Pennsylvania Press, 1960.

Scobie, Edward. *Black Britannia: A History of Blacks in Britain.* Chicago: Johnson Publishing Company, 1972.

Shepperson, George, and Price, Thomas. *Independent African: John Chilembwe and the Nyasaland Rising of 1916.* Edinburgh: The University Press, 1958.

Simons, H. J. and R. E. *Class and Colour in South Africa, 1850-1950.* Harmondsworth: Penguin, 1969.

Taylor, A. J. P. *The Trouble Makers.* London: Hamish Hamilton, 1957.

Thornton, A. P. *The Imperial Idea and Its Enemies.* New York: St. Martin's Press, 1959.

Thornbrugh, Emma Lou. *Timothy Thomas Fortune: Militant Journalist.* Chicago: University of Chicago Press, 1972.

Ullman, Victor. *Martin R. Delany: The Beginnings of Black Nationalism.* Boston: Beacon Press, 1971.

Weisbord, Robert G. *Ebony Kinship: Africa, Africans, and the Afro-American.* Westport, Conn.: Greenwood Press, 1973.

Whyte, Frederic. *A Life of W. T. Stead.* London: Cape, 1925.

Will, H. A. *Constitutional Change in the British West Indies, 1880-1903.* Oxford: Clarendon Press, 1970.

Williams, Eric. *A History of the People of Trinidad and Tobago.* New York: Praeger, 1964.

Williams, Lorraine, ed. *Africa and the Afro-American Experience.* Washington, D.C.: Howard University Press, 1973.

Wilson, Monica, and Thompson, L. *The Oxford History of South Africa.* New York: Oxford University Press, 1971.

Winks, Robin W. *The Blacks in Canada: A History.* New Haven: Yale University Press, 1971.

Wood, Donald. *Trinidad in Transition.* New York, London: Oxford University Press, 1968.

Wrong, Hume. *Government of the West Indies.* Oxford: Clarendon Press, 1923.

Articles

Contee, Clarence. "DuBois, The N.A.A.C.P., and the Pan-African Congress of 1919." *Journal of Negro History* 57 (January 1972): 13-28.

Elkins, W. F. "Hercules and the Society of Peoples of African Origin." *Caribbean Studies* (January 1972): 47-49.

Damas, Léon. "Price-Mars, Father of Haitianism." *Presence Africaine* 3-4 (June-September 1960): 166-178.

Geiss, Imanuel. "Notes on the Development of Pan-Africanism." *Journal of the Historical Society of Nigeria* 3 (June 1967): 719-740.

Lynch, Hollis R. "Pan-Negro Nationalism in the New World Before 1862." *Boston University Papers* 3 (1966): 149-179.

Nicol, Abioseh. "West Indians in West Africa" *Sierra Leone Studies* 13 (June 1960): 14-23.

Shepperson, George A. "Notes on Negro American Influences on the Emergence of African Nationalism." *Journal of African History* 1 (1960): 299-312.

——— ."Pan-Africanism and 'pan-Africanism': Some historical Notes." *Phylon* 23 (1962): 346-358.

Van de Ross, Richard. "The Founding of the African Peoples Organiza-

tion in Cape Town in 1903 and the Role of Dr. Abdurahman."
Manger Africana Library Notes 5 (1974-1975).
Wahle, Kathleen. "Alexander Crummell: Black Evangelist and Pan-
Negro Nationalist." *Phylon* 29 (Winter 1968): 388-395.

Index

ABOUT THE AUTHOR

Owen Charles Mathurin is a journalist, living in Trinidad. He has worked on various newspapers in Trinidad, England, and the United States. For ten years he was in the service of the government of Trinidad and Tobago in Port-of-Spain and Washington, D.C., first as the public relations officer in the Office of the Prime Minister, then as information and press attaché at the Embassy of Trinidad and Tobago in Washington, D.C. Owen Mathurin has been a member of many delegations from Trinidad and Tobago and has accompanied the Prime Minister on official visits.